Based on the Texas Essential Knowledge and Skills (TEKS)

STAAR

SUCCESS STRATEGIES
Grade 5
Reading

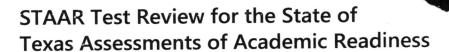

STAAR Test Review for the State of
Texas Assessments of Academic Readiness

Dear Future Exam Success Story:

First of all, **THANK YOU** for purchasing Mometrix study materials!

Second, congratulations! You are one of the few determined test-takers who are committed to doing whatever it takes to excel on your exam. **You have come to the right place.** We developed these study materials with one goal in mind: to deliver you the information you need in a format that's concise and easy to use.

In addition to optimizing your guide for the content of the test, we've outlined our recommended steps for breaking down the preparation process into small, attainable goals so you can make sure you stay on track.

We've also analyzed the entire test-taking process, identifying the most common pitfalls and showing how you can overcome them and be ready for any curveball the test throws you.

Standardized testing is one of the biggest obstacles on your road to success, which only increases the importance of doing well in the high-pressure, high-stakes environment of test day. Your results on this test could have a significant impact on your future, and this guide provides the information and practical advice to help you achieve your full potential on test day.

Your success is our success

We would love to hear from you! If you would like to share the story of your exam success or if you have any questions or comments in regard to our products, please contact us at **800-673-8175** or **support@mometrix.com**.

Thanks again for your business and we wish you continued success!

Sincerely,
The Mometrix Test Preparation Team

Need more help? Check out our flashcards at: http://MometrixFlashcards.com/STAAR

TABLE OF CONTENTS

Introduction

Thank you for purchasing this resource! You have made the choice to prepare yourself for a test that could have a huge impact on your future, and this guide is designed to help you be fully ready for test day. Obviously, it's important to have a solid understanding of the test material, but you also need to be prepared for the unique environment and stressors of the test, so that you can perform to the best of your abilities.

For this purpose, the first section that appears in this guide is the **Secret Keys**. We've devoted countless hours to meticulously researching what works and what doesn't, and we've boiled down our findings to the five most impactful steps you can take to improve your performance on the test. We start at the beginning with study planning and move through the preparation process, all the way to the testing strategies that will help you get the most out of what you know when you're finally sitting in front of the test.

We recommend that you start preparing for your test as far in advance as possible. However, if you've bought this guide as a last-minute study resource and only have a few days before your test, we recommend that you skip over the first two Secret Keys since they address a long-term study plan.

If you struggle with **test anxiety**, we strongly encourage you to check out our recommendations for how you can overcome it. Test anxiety is a formidable foe, but it can be beaten, and we want to make sure you have the tools you need to defeat it.

Secret Key #1 – Plan Big, Study Small

There's a lot riding on your performance. If you want to ace this test, you're going to need to keep your skills sharp and the material fresh in your mind. You need a plan that lets you review everything you need to know while still fitting in your schedule. We'll break this strategy down into three categories.

Information Organization

Start with the information you already have: the official test outline. From this, you can make a complete list of all the concepts you need to cover before the test. Organize these concepts into groups that can be studied together, and create a list of any related vocabulary you need to learn so you can brush up on any difficult terms. You'll want to keep this vocabulary list handy once you actually start studying since you may need to add to it along the way.

Time Management

Once you have your set of study concepts, decide how to spread them out over the time you have left before the test. Break your study plan into small, clear goals so you have a manageable task for each day and know exactly what you're doing. Then just focus on one small step at a time. When you manage your time this way, you don't need to spend hours at a time studying. Studying a small block of content for a short period each day helps you retain information better and avoid stressing over how much you have left to do. You can relax knowing that you have a plan to cover everything in time. In order for this strategy to be effective though, you have to start studying early and stick to your schedule. Avoid the exhaustion and futility that comes from last-minute cramming!

Study Environment

The environment you study in has a big impact on your learning. Studying in a coffee shop, while probably more enjoyable, is not likely to be as fruitful as studying in a quiet room. It's important to keep distractions to a minimum. You're only planning to study for a short block of time, so make the most of it. Don't pause to check your phone or get up to find a snack. It's also important to **avoid multitasking**. Research has consistently shown that multitasking will make your studying dramatically less effective. Your study area should also be comfortable and well-lit so you don't have the distraction of straining your eyes or sitting on an uncomfortable chair.

The time of day you study is also important. You want to be rested and alert. Don't wait until just before bedtime. Study when you'll be most likely to comprehend and remember. Even better, if you know what time of day your test will be, set that time aside for study. That way your brain will be used to working on that subject at that specific time and you'll have a better chance of recalling information.

Finally, it can be helpful to team up with others who are studying for the same test. Your actual studying should be done in as isolated an environment as possible, but the work of organizing the information and setting up the study plan can be divided up. In between study sessions, you can discuss with your teammates the concepts that you're all studying and quiz each other on the details. Just be sure that your teammates are as serious about the test as you are. If you find that your study time is being replaced with social time, you might need to find a new team.

Secret Key #2 – Make Your Studying Count

You're devoting a lot of time and effort to preparing for this test, so you want to be absolutely certain it will pay off. This means doing more than just reading the content and hoping you can remember it on test day. It's important to make every minute of study count. There are two main areas you can focus on to make your studying count:

Retention

It doesn't matter how much time you study if you can't remember the material. You need to make sure you are retaining the concepts. To check your retention of the information you're learning, try recalling it at later times with minimal prompting. Try carrying around flashcards and glance at one or two from time to time or ask a friend who's also studying for the test to quiz you.

To enhance your retention, look for ways to put the information into practice so that you can apply it rather than simply recalling it. If you're using the information in practical ways, it will be much easier to remember. Similarly, it helps to solidify a concept in your mind if you're not only reading it to yourself but also explaining it to someone else. Ask a friend to let you teach them about a concept you're a little shaky on (or speak aloud to an imaginary audience if necessary). As you try to summarize, define, give examples, and answer your friend's questions, you'll understand the concepts better and they will stay with you longer. Finally, step back for a big picture view and ask yourself how each piece of information fits with the whole subject. When you link the different concepts together and see them working together as a whole, it's easier to remember the individual components.

Finally, practice showing your work on any multi-step problems, even if you're just studying. Writing out each step you take to solve a problem will help solidify the process in your mind, and you'll be more likely to remember it during the test.

Modality

Modality simply refers to the means or method by which you study. Choosing a study modality that fits your own individual learning style is crucial. No two people learn best in exactly the same way, so it's important to know your strengths and use them to your advantage.

For example, if you learn best by visualization, focus on visualizing a concept in your mind and draw an image or a diagram. Try color-coding your notes, illustrating them, or creating symbols that will trigger your mind to recall a learned concept. If you learn best by hearing or discussing information, find a study partner who learns the same way or read aloud to yourself. Think about how to put the information in your own words. Imagine that you are giving a lecture on the topic and record yourself so you can listen to it later.

For any learning style, flashcards can be helpful. Organize the information so you can take advantage of spare moments to review. Underline key words or phrases. Use different colors for different categories. Mnemonic devices (such as creating a short list in which every item starts with the same letter) can also help with retention. Find what works best for you and use it to store the information in your mind most effectively and easily.

Secret Key #3 – Practice the Right Way

Your success on test day depends not only on how many hours you put into preparing, but also on whether you prepared the right way. It's good to check along the way to see if your studying is paying off. One of the most effective ways to do this is by taking practice tests to evaluate your progress. Practice tests are useful because they show exactly where you need to improve. Every time you take a practice test, pay special attention to these three groups of questions:

- The questions you got wrong
- The questions you had to guess on, even if you guessed right
- The questions you found difficult or slow to work through

This will show you exactly what your weak areas are, and where you need to devote more study time. Ask yourself why each of these questions gave you trouble. Was it because you didn't understand the material? Was it because you didn't remember the vocabulary? Do you need more repetitions on this type of question to build speed and confidence? Dig into those questions and figure out how you can strengthen your weak areas as you go back to review the material.

Additionally, many practice tests have a section explaining the answer choices. It can be tempting to read the explanation and think that you now have a good understanding of the concept. However, an explanation likely only covers part of the question's broader context. Even if the explanation makes sense, **go back and investigate** every concept related to the question until you're positive you have a thorough understanding.

As you go along, keep in mind that the practice test is just that: practice. Memorizing these questions and answers will not be very helpful on the actual test because it is unlikely to have any of the same exact questions. If you only know the right answers to the sample questions, you won't be prepared for the real thing. **Study the concepts** until you understand them fully, and then you'll be able to answer any question that shows up on the test.

It's important to wait on the practice tests until you're ready. If you take a test on your first day of study, you may be overwhelmed by the amount of material covered and how much you need to learn. Work up to it gradually.

On test day, you'll need to be prepared for answering questions, managing your time, and using the test-taking strategies you've learned. It's a lot to balance, like a mental marathon that will have a big impact on your future. Like training for a marathon, you'll need to start slowly and work your way up. When test day arrives, you'll be ready.

Start with the strategies you've read in the first two Secret Keys—plan your course and study in the way that works best for you. If you have time, consider using multiple study resources to get different approaches to the same concepts. It can be helpful to see difficult concepts from more than one angle. Then find a good source for practice tests. Many times, the test website will suggest potential study resources or provide sample tests.

Practice Test Strategy

If you're able to find at least three practice tests, we recommend this strategy:

Untimed and Open-Book Practice

Take the first test with no time constraints and with your notes and study guide handy. Take your time and focus on applying the strategies you've learned.

Timed and Open-Book Practice

Take the second practice test open-book as well, but set a timer and practice pacing yourself to finish in time.

Timed and Closed-Book Practice

Take any other practice tests as if it were test day. Set a timer and put away your study materials. Sit at a table or desk in a quiet room, imagine yourself at the testing center, and answer questions as quickly and accurately as possible.

Keep repeating timed and closed-book tests on a regular basis until you run out of practice tests or it's time for the actual test. Your mind will be ready for the schedule and stress of test day, and you'll be able to focus on recalling the material you've learned.

Secret Key #4 – Pace Yourself

Once you're fully prepared for the material on the test, your biggest challenge on test day will be managing your time. Just knowing that the clock is ticking can make you panic even if you have plenty of time left. Work on pacing yourself so you can build confidence against the time constraints of the exam. Pacing is a difficult skill to master, especially in a high-pressure environment, so **practice is vital**.

Set time expectations for your pace based on how much time is available. For example, if a section has 60 questions and the time limit is 30 minutes, you know you have to average 30 seconds or less per question in order to answer them all. Although 30 seconds is the hard limit, set 25 seconds per question as your goal, so you reserve extra time to spend on harder questions. When you budget extra time for the harder questions, you no longer have any reason to stress when those questions take longer to answer.

Don't let this time expectation distract you from working through the test at a calm, steady pace, but keep it in mind so you don't spend too much time on any one question. Recognize that taking extra time on one question you don't understand may keep you from answering two that you do understand later in the test. If your time limit for a question is up and you're still not sure of the answer, mark it and move on, and come back to it later if the time and the test format allow. If the testing format doesn't allow you to return to earlier questions, just make an educated guess; then put it out of your mind and move on.

On the easier questions, be careful not to rush. It may seem wise to hurry through them so you have more time for the challenging ones, but it's not worth missing one if you know the concept and just didn't take the time to read the question fully. Work efficiently but make sure you understand the question and have looked at all of the answer choices, since more than one may seem right at first.

Even if you're paying attention to the time, you may find yourself a little behind at some point. You should speed up to get back on track, but do so wisely. Don't panic; just take a few seconds less on each question until you're caught up. Don't guess without thinking, but do look through the answer choices and eliminate any you know are wrong. If you can get down to two choices, it is often worthwhile to guess from those. Once you've chosen an answer, move on and don't dwell on any that you skipped or had to hurry through. If a question was taking too long, chances are it was one of the harder ones, so you weren't as likely to get it right anyway.

On the other hand, if you find yourself getting ahead of schedule, it may be beneficial to slow down a little. The more quickly you work, the more likely you are to make a careless mistake that will affect your score. You've budgeted time for each question, so don't be afraid to spend that time. Practice an efficient but careful pace to get the most out of the time you have.

Secret Key #5 – Have a Plan for Guessing

When you're taking the test, you may find yourself stuck on a question. Some of the answer choices seem better than others, but you don't see the one answer choice that is obviously correct. What do you do?

The scenario described above is very common, yet most test takers have not effectively prepared for it. Developing and practicing a plan for guessing may be one of the single most effective uses of your time as you get ready for the exam.

In developing your plan for guessing, there are three questions to address:

- When should you start the guessing process?
- How should you narrow down the choices?
- Which answer should you choose?

When to Start the Guessing Process

Unless your plan for guessing is to select C every time (which, despite its merits, is not what we recommend), you need to leave yourself enough time to apply your answer elimination strategies. Since you have a limited amount of time for each question, that means that if you're going to give yourself the best shot at guessing correctly, you have to decide quickly whether or not you will guess.

Of course, the best-case scenario is that you don't have to guess at all, so first, see if you can answer the question based on your knowledge of the subject and basic reasoning skills. Focus on the key words in the question and try to jog your memory of related topics. Give yourself a chance to bring the knowledge to mind, but once you realize that you don't have (or you can't access) the knowledge you need to answer the question, it's time to start the guessing process.

It's almost always better to start the guessing process too early than too late. It only takes a few seconds to remember something and answer the question from knowledge. Carefully eliminating wrong answer choices takes longer. Plus, going through the process of eliminating answer choices can actually help jog your memory.

Summary: Start the guessing process as soon as you decide that you can't answer the question based on your knowledge.

How to Narrow Down the Choices

The next chapter in this book (**Test-Taking Strategies**) includes a wide range of strategies for how to approach questions and how to look for answer choices to eliminate. You will definitely want to read those carefully, practice them, and figure out which ones work best for you. Here though, we're going to address a mindset rather than a particular strategy.

Your chances of guessing an answer correctly depend on how many options you are choosing from.

How many choices you have	How likely you are to guess correctly
5	20%
4	25%
3	33%
2	50%
1	100%

You can see from this chart just how valuable it is to be able to eliminate incorrect answers and make an educated guess, but there are two things that many test takers do that cause them to miss out on the benefits of guessing:

- Accidentally eliminating the correct answer
- Selecting an answer based on an impression

We'll look at the first one here, and the second one in the next section.

To avoid accidentally eliminating the correct answer, we recommend a thought exercise called **the $5 challenge**. In this challenge, you only eliminate an answer choice from contention if you are willing to bet $5 on it being wrong. Why $5? Five dollars is a small but not insignificant amount of money. It's an amount you could afford to lose but wouldn't want to throw away. And while losing $5 once might not hurt too much, doing it twenty times will set you back $100. In the same way, each small decision you make—eliminating a choice here, guessing on a question there—won't by itself impact your score very much, but when you put them all together, they can make a big difference. By holding each answer choice elimination decision to a higher standard, you can reduce the risk of accidentally eliminating the correct answer.

The $5 challenge can also be applied in a positive sense: If you are willing to bet $5 that an answer choice *is* correct, go ahead and mark it as correct.

Summary: Only eliminate an answer choice if you are willing to bet $5 that it is wrong.

Which Answer to Choose

You're taking the test. You've run into a hard question and decided you'll have to guess. You've eliminated all the answer choices you're willing to bet $5 on. Now you have to pick an answer. Why do we even need to talk about this? Why can't you just pick whichever one you feel like when the time comes?

The answer to these questions is that if you don't come into the test with a plan, you'll rely on your impression to select an answer choice, and if you do that, you risk falling into a trap. The test writers know that everyone who takes their test will be guessing on some of the questions, so they intentionally write wrong answer choices to seem plausible. You still have to pick an answer though, and if the wrong answer choices are designed to look right, how can you ever be sure that you're not falling for their trap? The best solution we've found to this dilemma is to take the decision out of your hands entirely. Here is the process we recommend:

Once you've eliminated any choices that you are confident (willing to bet $5) are wrong, select the first remaining choice as your answer.

Whether you choose to select the first remaining choice, the second, or the last, the important thing is that you use some preselected standard. Using this approach guarantees that you will not be enticed into selecting an answer choice that looks right, because you are not basing your decision on how the answer choices look.

This is not meant to make you question your knowledge. Instead, it is to help you recognize the difference between your knowledge and your impressions. There's a huge difference between thinking an answer is right because of what you know, and thinking an answer is right because it looks or sounds like it should be right.

Summary: To ensure that your selection is appropriately random, make a predetermined selection from among all answer choices you have not eliminated.

Test-Taking Strategies

This section contains a list of test-taking strategies that you may find helpful as you work through the test. By taking what you know and applying logical thought, you can maximize your chances of answering any question correctly!

It is very important to realize that every question is different and every person is different: no single strategy will work on every question, and no single strategy will work for every person. That's why we've included all of them here, so you can try them out and determine which ones work best for different types of questions and which ones work best for you.

Question Strategies

Read Carefully

Read the question and answer choices carefully. Don't miss the question because you misread the terms. You have plenty of time to read each question thoroughly and make sure you understand what is being asked. Yet a happy medium must be attained, so don't waste too much time. You must read carefully, but efficiently.

Contextual Clues

Look for contextual clues. If the question includes a word you are not familiar with, look at the immediate context for some indication of what the word might mean. Contextual clues can often give you all the information you need to decipher the meaning of an unfamiliar word. Even if you can't determine the meaning, you may be able to narrow down the possibilities enough to make a solid guess at the answer to the question.

Prefixes

If you're having trouble with a word in the question or answer choices, try dissecting it. Take advantage of every clue that the word might include. Prefixes and suffixes can be a huge help. Usually they allow you to determine a basic meaning. Pre- means before, post- means after, pro - is positive, de- is negative. From prefixes and suffixes, you can get an idea of the general meaning of the word and try to put it into context.

Hedge Words

Watch out for critical hedge words, such as *likely, may, can, sometimes, often, almost, mostly, usually, generally, rarely*, and *sometimes*. Question writers insert these hedge phrases to cover every possibility. Often an answer choice will be wrong simply because it leaves no room for exception. Be on guard for answer choices that have definitive words such as *exactly* and *always*.

Switchback Words

Stay alert for *switchbacks*. These are the words and phrases frequently used to alert you to shifts in thought. The most common switchback words are *but, although*, and *however*. Others include *nevertheless, on the other hand, even though, while, in spite of, despite, regardless of*. Switchback words are important to catch because they can change the direction of the question or an answer choice.

Face Value

When in doubt, use common sense. Accept the situation in the problem at face value. Don't read too much into it. These problems will not require you to make wild assumptions. If you have to go beyond creativity and warp time or space in order to have an answer choice fit the question, then you should move on and consider the other answer choices. These are normal problems rooted in reality. The applicable relationship or explanation may not be readily apparent, but it is there for you to figure out. Use your common sense to interpret anything that isn't clear.

Answer Choice Strategies

Answer Selection

The most thorough way to pick an answer choice is to identify and eliminate wrong answers until only one is left, then confirm it is the correct answer. Sometimes an answer choice may immediately seem right, but be careful. The test writers will usually put more than one reasonable answer choice on each question, so take a second to read all of them and make sure that the other choices are not equally obvious. As long as you have time left, it is better to read every answer choice than to pick the first one that looks right without checking the others.

Answer Choice Families

An answer choice family consists of two (in rare cases, three) answer choices that are very similar in construction and cannot all be true at the same time. If you see two answer choices that are direct opposites or parallels, one of them is usually the correct answer. For instance, if one answer choice says that quantity x increases and another either says that quantity x decreases (opposite) or says that quantity y increases (parallel), then those answer choices would fall into the same family. An answer choice that doesn't match the construction of the answer choice family is more likely to be incorrect. Most questions will not have answer choice families, but when they do appear, you should be prepared to recognize them.

Eliminate Answers

Eliminate answer choices as soon as you realize they are wrong, but make sure you consider all possibilities. If you are eliminating answer choices and realize that the last one you are left with is also wrong, don't panic. Start over and consider each choice again. There may be something you missed the first time that you will realize on the second pass.

Avoid Fact Traps

Don't be distracted by an answer choice that is factually true but doesn't answer the question. You are looking for the choice that answers the question. Stay focused on what the question is asking for so you don't accidentally pick an answer that is true but incorrect. Always go back to the question and make sure the answer choice you've selected actually answers the question and is not merely a true statement.

Extreme Statements

In general, you should avoid answers that put forth extreme actions as standard practice or proclaim controversial ideas as established fact. An answer choice that states the "process should be used in certain situations, if..." is much more likely to be correct than one that states the "process should be discontinued completely." The first is a calm rational statement and doesn't even make a definitive, uncompromising stance, using a hedge word *if* to provide wiggle room, whereas the second choice is a radical idea and far more extreme.

Benchmark

As you read through the answer choices and you come across one that seems to answer the question well, mentally select that answer choice. This is not your final answer, but it's the one that will help you evaluate the other answer choices. The one that you selected is your benchmark or standard for judging each of the other answer choices. Every other answer choice must be compared to your benchmark. That choice is correct until proven otherwise by another answer choice beating it. If you find a better answer, then that one becomes your new benchmark. Once you've decided that no other choice answers the question as well as your benchmark, you have your final answer.

Predict the Answer

Before you even start looking at the answer choices, it is often best to try to predict the answer. When you come up with the answer on your own, it is easier to avoid distractions and traps because you will know exactly what to look for. The right answer choice is unlikely to be word-for-word what you came up with, but it should be a close match. Even if you are confident that you have the right answer, you should still take the time to read each option before moving on.

General Strategies

Tough Questions

If you are stumped on a problem or it appears too hard or too difficult, don't waste time. Move on! Remember though, if you can quickly check for obviously incorrect answer choices, your chances of guessing correctly are greatly improved. Before you completely give up, at least try to knock out a couple of possible answers. Eliminate what you can and then guess at the remaining answer choices before moving on.

Check Your Work

Since you will probably not know every term listed and the answer to every question, it is important that you get credit for the ones that you do know. Don't miss any questions through careless mistakes. If at all possible, try to take a second to look back over your answer selection and make sure you've selected the correct answer choice and haven't made a costly careless mistake (such as marking an answer choice that you didn't mean to mark). This quick double check should more than pay for itself in caught mistakes for the time it costs.

Pace Yourself

It's easy to be overwhelmed when you're looking at a page full of questions; your mind is confused and full of random thoughts, and the clock is ticking down faster than you would like. Calm down and maintain the pace that you have set for yourself. Especially as you get down to the last few minutes of the test, don't let the small numbers on the clock make you panic. As long as you are on track by monitoring your pace, you are guaranteed to have time for each question.

Don't Rush

It is very easy to make errors when you are in a hurry. Maintaining a fast pace in answering questions is pointless if it makes you miss questions that you would have gotten right otherwise. Test writers like to include distracting information and wrong answers that seem right. Taking a little extra time to avoid careless mistakes can make all the difference in your test score. Find a pace that allows you to be confident in the answers that you select.

Keep Moving

Panicking will not help you pass the test, so do your best to stay calm and keep moving. Taking deep breaths and going through the answer elimination steps you practiced can help to break through a stress barrier and keep your pace.

Final Notes

The combination of a solid foundation of content knowledge and the confidence that comes from practicing your plan for applying that knowledge is the key to maximizing your performance on test day. As your foundation of content knowledge is built up and strengthened, you'll find that the strategies included in this chapter become more and more effective in helping you quickly sift through the distractions and traps of the test to isolate the correct answer.

Now it's time to move on to the test content chapters of this book, but be sure to keep your goal in mind. As you read, think about how you will be able to apply this information on the test. If you've already seen sample questions for the test and you have an idea of the question format and style, try to come up with questions of your own that you can answer based on what you're reading. This will give you valuable practice applying your knowledge in the same ways you can expect to on test day.

Good luck and good studying!

- 14 -

Reading Assessment

Determining word meaning

Root word and affix

A root word is the base word, before an affix, in the form of a prefix, infix, or suffix, is added onto it. Many affixes in the English language come from Latin or Greek origins. A prefix is added onto the beginning of a root word, an infix is added into the middle, and a suffix is added onto the end of a root word. By looking at the meaning of a root word and the meaning of any affixes added to it, the reader can figure out the approximate meaning of the word. For example, the root word 'like' means to enjoy and the prefix 'dis-' means not. The reader can therefore understand that the full word 'dislike' means to not enjoy.

A reader can use root words and affixes to figure out the general meaning of an unknown word. Knowing root words and affixes is helpful on tests where analogies are made using unfamiliar words. By figuring out the general meaning of a new word, a tester can figure out the general relationship presented between two words.

In the word unhappy, the affix 'un-' means not. By adding the prefix 'un-' onto a word, the word attains its opposite meaning. Some other words containing the affix 'un-' that add the opposite meaning to the word include: unfair, unable, and uninformed. By adding an affix, as in a prefix or suffix, onto a word, the meaning of the word in its entirety is altered.

Context clues

The term *context clues* refers to words or phrases found in sentences surrounding an unknown word. Context clues may include examples of the unknown word, synonyms, antonyms, definitions, or contrasting information. By using context clues in the surrounding sentences, the reader can figure out approximately what the word means. A context clue indicating an example may contain the unknown word(s) including the phrase 'such as,' a dash, or a colon before stated information. A synonym is a word with a similar meaning to the unknown word, whereas an antonym is a word with the opposite meaning. A definition will state exactly what the unknown word means. Contrasting information will include facts that are different from the unknown word.

Example 1: Based on context, determine the meaning of *hearing* in the following sentence:

The *hearing* to decide whether a trial is needed will be held on April 5th at the Edmonton County Courthouse.

In the example, the word *hearing* is a homonym, in other words, it has different meanings when used in different contexts, even though it's spelled the same. In the sentence, the word *hearing* clearly refers to an event that determines whether a trial is needed. The fact that the event is set to occur at the Edmonton County Courthouse lets the reader know that a *hearing* is a legal matter. The reader then knows, from the context of the sentence, that the homonym does not refer to perceiving sound, an alternative meaning if used in a different context.

Example 2: Using context clues, determine the meaning of the word *staggered* in the following sentence:

As soon as he heard his Father's voice, he jumped up from his seat to open the door, but, as he did so, he *staggered* and fell headlong to the floor.

- 15 -

Context clues are words in the sentence and surrounding sentences that help the reader to figure out the meaning of an unknown word. In the example, the word *staggered* refers to the action the character was taking before he "fell headlong to the floor". The reader knows that the character was on his feet, but that he did not have his balance. The reader can therefore conclude that the word *staggered* means to move unsteadily. By using the information around a word in a sentence, the overall meaning of a word in context can be understood. Using context clues to figure out meaning can be helpful when learning a new set of vocabulary words or reading a difficult text. The dictionary definition of a word can always be looked-up to verify intended meaning.

Dictionary, Glossary, and Thesaurus

One tool that can be used to build word meanings is the dictionary. A dictionary contains words listed alphabetically. It tells each word's meaning. It also tells the word's part of speech. Dictionaries can be books or be online. Glossaries are like dictionaries, but they are smaller than dictionaries. Glossaries list words alphabetically. They tell each word's meaning. They are found at the back of books, and they list words in the books. A thesaurus is a reference book that gives synonyms of words. It is different from a dictionary because a thesaurus does not give definitions, only lists of synonyms. A thesaurus can be helpful in finding the meaning of an unfamiliar word when reading. If the meaning of a synonym is known, then the meaning of the unfamiliar word will be known. The other time a thesaurus is helpful is when writing. Using a thesaurus helps authors to vary their word choice.

Homonyms, homophones, and homographs

A *multiple-meaning word* has different definitions, depending on the contextual use of the word. A multiple-meaning word is also called a homonym. It is defined as a word that has more than one meaning, but is spelled and pronounced the same for all of them. For example, the word 'saw' can have two different meanings: having sighted in the past or a tool used to cut wood. Homophones are words that are pronounced the same, but may be spelled differently. An example of two homophones would be heir (someone due to inherit an estate) and air (the invisible substance people breathe). Homographs are words that are spelled the same, but may be pronounced differently. An example of a homograph is the word *row*, which is pronounced one way when used to mean a horizontal grouping and is pronounced another way when used to mean an argument.

Inference

An inference is a conclusion or generalization that the reader makes based on the information provided within a text. Certain facts are included to help a reader come to a specific conclusion. For example, a story may open with a man trudging through the snow on a cold winter day, dragging a sled behind him. The reader can logically infer from the setting of the story that the man is wearing heavy winter clothes in order to stay warm. Information is implied based on the setting of a story, which is why setting is an important element of the text. If the same man in the example was trudging down a beach on a hot summer day, dragging a surf board behind him, the reader would assume that the man is not wearing heavy clothes. The reader makes inferences based on their own experiences and the information presented to them in the story.

Example 1

Read the following sentence and draw a conclusion based upon the information presented:

"You know the reason Mother proposed not having any presents this Christmas was because it is going to be a hard winter for everyone; and she thinks we ought not to spend

- 16 -

money for pleasure, when our men are suffering so in the army." (from *Little Women* by Louisa May Alcott, p. 3)

Based on the information in the sentence, the reader can conclude, or infer, that the men are away at war while the women are still at home. The pronoun 'our' gives a clue to the reader that the character is speaking about men she knows. In addition, the reader can assume that the character is speaking to a brother or sister, since the term Mother is used by the character while speaking to another person. The reader can also come to the conclusion that the characters celebrate Christmas, since it is mentioned in the context of the sentence. In the sentence, the Mother is presented as an unselfish character who is opinionated and thinks about the well-being of other people.

Example 2

Read the following two sentences and draw a conclusion based on the text:

> Sarah worked hard on her science project. Her presentation of the science project to the class went well.

Based on the two sentences, the reader can conclude that Sarah will receive a high grade on her science project. The reader knows that Sarah put a great deal of time and effort into her project and that the actual presentation of the project was successful. Based on these facts, the reader can assume that the teacher will appreciate and reward Sarah's effort. This conclusion can be drawn based on the reader's knowledge of how high grades are obtained and their own previous experience with school projects. The reader can assume that Sarah's assessment of her presentation is accurate, that the presentation did indeed conform to high expectations. When a conclusion is drawn based on information the reader is given in a text, the conclusion is called an *inference*.

Example 3

Draw a conclusion based on the following sentence from *The Adventures of Tom Sawyer* by Mark Twain:

> He had discovered a great law of human action, without knowing it—namely, that in order to make a man or a boy covet a thing, it is only necessary to make the thing difficult to attain.

The reader can conclude from the sentence that the character did not set out to learn something, but through an action, the character learned that people will want what is hard to attain. The character learned a fact about human nature: that a person will value something more if they have to work hard for it, than if it is simply given to them. The word *covet* means to desire, which the character learns can be manipulated by making an item or an outcome more difficult to grasp. In everyday life, this could apply toward taking a hard test and doing well. If someone studies for a hard test and does well, the person will value their score more than if the test was very easy and he or she did not study for the test.

Comparison and contrast

Comparison and contrast involves looking at the similarities and differences between ideas and topics of debate. Ideas may vary in complexity, in addition to their main point. Topics of debate, or issues, may have pros and cons. For example, two essays may take different points of view on whether or not a new school needs to be built. By comparing the positive and negative aspects of each view, the reader can better understand how the viewpoints are similar and different. If the

- 17 -

reader needs to make a decision on an issue, he or she may list what they like about an idea and what they dislike about an idea. This helps the reader to come to a final conclusion about an idea or issue of debate.

<u>Example</u>

Read the following two viewpoints and compare and contrast how the two viewpoints are similar and different:

> (1) Basketball is the best sport to play, because a participant can be part of a team and excel individually.

> (2) In basketball, players must work together to execute plays and achieve points for the team.

In the first viewpoint, the author states that basketball is the best sport to play, whereas in the second viewpoint, the author simply states how the game is played. The first viewpoint also refers to an individual player's performance, while the second viewpoint focuses on the fact that the team needs to score points together in order to win the game. The first viewpoint is trying to convince the reader, while the second viewpoint is explaining how the game is played. Yes, an individual may excel at scoring points, as indicated in the first viewpoint, but the second viewpoint emphasizes the fact that plays need to be done together in order to score points for the entire team. Two differing viewpoints will often overlap in relation to the topic that they are discussing.

Origin myths

An origin myth is a myth that claims to describe the origin of some feature in the natural world or the way in which some new reality came to be. Most ancient cultures have their own origin myths that explain their creation and justify their established order by attributing its existing to sacred forces. Many origin myths share similar features and themes with those from other cultures.

Historical and Cultural Setting

Historical context influences literature in a number of ways. The style of the author's writing can be impacted by the historical period during which it was written (e.g., Dickens wrote at a time when authors were paid by the word; this is why his novels are so long). Obviously, the setting of the book includes its historical context. In addition, dialect may be a function of the historical period of the book. When a reader understands the historical context of a particular book, he or she can have a deeper understanding of the novel. Knowing about the time period in which the author wrote, as well as the time period discussed in the novel, helps the reader understand some of the author's choices, including character motivations.

<u>Example</u>

Slavery used to be the norm in Southern states. One of the major ways in which the historical context of slavery impacted literature coming out of the South was the birth of the slave narrative. Slaves wanted to have their experiences documented. After the Civil War, former slaves wrote their stories. These slave narratives have given historians valuable firsthand accounts of life in the South. From a literary perspective, slave narratives are one of the most important genres of African-American writing. Slavery influenced literature by delving into themes of power, racial injustice, and equality. Literature from this time period can help the reader better understand the perspectives and experiences of the slaves themselves, as well as the slave holders.

Purpose

<u>Example 1</u>

Read the following sentence and state the author's point in writing the sentence, whether it is to inform, entertain, persuade, or state an opinion:

> The new city law makes it illegal to use cell phones to send text messages while driving.

The purpose of this sentence is to inform the reader. The sentence does not state an opinion on the topic, nor is it meant to entertain the reader. The sentence also does not persuade the reader to accept a certain point of view. The sentence gives information to the reader that they need to know in order to avoid breaking the law.

<u>Example 2</u>

Read the following sentence from *Morte d'Arthur* by Sir Thomas Malory and state the author's purpose in writing the sentence: whether it is to inform, entertain, persuade, or state an opinion:

But Arthur was still only a baby, not two years old, and Merlin knew it would be no use yet to proclaim him king.

The purpose of the sentence is to entertain the reader. The sentence does not tell the reader important information about a specific topic, it is simply used as part of a greater fictional story meant for entertainment. The sentence does not persuade the reader to accept a certain point of view, nor does it state an opinion.

When an author wishes to persuade the reader to accept a certain point of view, evidence is used to back-up a claim. If the author wants to state an opinion, that opinion is included within the text. Sentences that are meant to inform contain facts that the reader needs to know and are not often found in fictional stories.

Sound effects in poetry

Poets use alliteration, internal rhyme, onomatopoeia and rhyme scheme to help readers understand poems. Alliteration is when the author repeats the same sound in the first syllable of a series of words or phrases of words. An example of this would be found in the line "seven swimming swans slid gracefully by". Internal rhyme is when a rhyme occurs in a single verse. An onomatopoeia is a word that imitates the sound that is makes, such as "meow", "oink" or "ding". Rhyme scheme is the pattern of rhymes between the lines in a poem or in a song. Often poets will write a verse so that the ending word of every other line rhymes. These sound effects increase the flow of the poem and help to involve the reader's emotions.

Text structure

<u>Cause and effect</u>

The term *cause and effect* means when one event happens in a text, another event occurs because of it. The term *chronology* refers to the order of events over time. For example, a text may discuss the school policy that, when a student is late to school too many times, they receive a detention. The student being late too many times is the cause and the detention is the effect. Chronology of events in a story can occur over a short, or extended, period of time. For example, if a text discusses the rise of the Roman Empire, it may include the rulers of the Roman Empire over time and any changes that occurred during each ruler's time in power.

Compare and Contrast

Comparison and contrast involves showing similarities and differences between items or events. As an example the author may write about a Compare and Contrast about cats and dogs. They can start by giving a brief description of the two. Then they will want to point out all of the similarities, such as; they both have tails, and both are kept as pets. Next they will explain the differences, such as; dogs are canines, while cats are felines. They will try to provide as much detail as possible about both the similarities and the differences.

Example

Identify the text structure that is used in the following sentence from *Morte d'Arthur* by Sir Thomas Malory:

The king had given his promise, so he was obliged to agree.

The text structure of cause and effect is used in this sentence. The cause in the sentence is that the king gave his promise, and the effect is that he had to agree. Information can also be organized according to chronological order, spatial order, order of importance, or organized by description. Chronological order means the order of events as they occur over time. Spatial order is the way things are placed in a location, such as the way people are seated around a table. Order of importance is used to place the most important information first, with the least important information last (or vice-versa). Description is used to organize information according to what it looks and feels like.

Main idea and supporting details

The main idea(s) in a passage are usually located in the first paragraph or two of text. Having the main idea(s) near the beginning of the passage allows the author to grab the reader's attention and let them know what the rest of the passage will discuss. To find the main idea(s) in a passage, there are questions the reader can ask while reading: What is this passage about? What does the author want the reader to know about the topic? The supporting details will provide evidence that the main idea is correct and are found in the body of a passage. The supporting details often provide examples of the main idea. For example, a passage may contain the main idea: "Ellis Island was an entry-point to America for many immigrants during the Industrial Revolution." A supporting detail for the main idea may be "Immigrants were examined for contagious diseases at Ellis Island before being granted entry to America."

Example

Determine the main idea the following sentence tells the reader and indicate what details support the main idea:

Her breath billowed out in clouds of white and disappeared into the quiet air.

The main idea is what the author wants the reader to understand about the text. Details help to explain or support that main idea. A main idea usually states the point of an entire essay, article, or book, but can be simply stated in one sentence. The main idea in the sentence above is that a girl is outside in the cold. Details to support this statement include the word 'her,' showing that the character is a girl, and 'clouds of white,' which indicate that the air is cold. In order to conclude that the girl is out in the cold, the reader needs to understand that breath can be seen when the air is cold.

- 20 -

Text evidence

The term text evidence refers to information included in a text that supports the main point of the paper, from which a reader can draw conclusions or generalizations. The author will deliberately include key points that serve as supporting details for the main point of a paper. For example, the main point of a paper may state: The average yearly rainfall in the city has risen by 2 inches per year since 1999. The paper would go on to include the amount of rainfall for each month or season and any contributing factors that may be causing an increase in yearly rainfall. Additional facts, or text evidence to support the point that yearly rainfall is rising in the city would help to prove that the author's main point is correct.

Main point and opposite point of view

Read the following topic sentence. Describe what the opposite point of view would include:

> The new bike path at Primer School provides families in the community with a safe opportunity to get some fresh air on the weekends.

This topic sentence could be taken in several different directions. The main focus of the sentence is that the bike path is safe and allows for families to get out and enjoy some fresh air on the weekends. The opposite point of view may state that the new bike path is unsafe and the air is polluted. An example of a topic sentence with the opposite point of view may state: The new bike path at Primer School is unsafe for families in the community to travel on the weekends and goes through a polluted area.

When looking for the main point in a sentence, look for keywords that define the sentence. In the sentence about the bike path, we know that the path is new, seems safe, and has fresh air. By changing around these keywords, the entire meaning of the sentence can be shifted.

Plot

The term *plot* refers to the series of events that take place in a story. The events in a story may take place in one location or many, in a short amount of time or over many years. Every story is different. A story always has to start somewhere, however and the first event in a story signals the beginning of the plot. Two characters may be simply talking at the opening of a story, which is the first step in the plot of the story. The characters may then hear a loud noise and rush outdoors, which is the next event that takes place in the plot of the story. Stories may vary in length from half a page to novel-length, but they all follow a progression of events that the author winds together to form the plot.

Plot sequence
Read the following plot and analyze what the missing event is in the plot sequence:

> Sarita went to the store to buy eggs for her mother. She bought the eggs and got back on her bicycle to bring the eggs home. Her mother was angry that the eggs were all broken.

The reader has to guess based on the plot sequence what happened between events. The reader knows that Sarita got on her bicycle to go home. The reader also knows that the eggs were broken when she arrived at the house. Based on the context, the reader can assume that Sarita fell off her bicycle or dropped the eggs on the way home, causing them to all be broken when she arrived. The reader can assume that Sarita would have noticed if the eggs were already broken in the store. Plot

- 21 -

often follows a logical sequence of events, but sometimes it is difficult to decide what actually happened between two events. In the example, the reader can logically assume that the eggs were broken on the way home.

Conflict

Conflict creates the basis for the plot of a story. A conflict may be between characters, a character and their own mind, or an outside influence. The main point of a conflict is that there is a problem that needs to be resolved. The problem may be a disagreement or an obstacle that has arisen and needs to be overcome.

A conflict needs to be based on an unresolved issue that either arises due to circumstance, a series of events, or something that has happened in the past. For example, two families may be feuding over land that the families acquired centuries ago and the conflict may be ongoing up to a given point in the story.

Example 1

Read the following sentence and explain the main conflict between the two characters:

> Joe stared angrily at Jamie's retreating back as Jamie raced away down the field with Joe's soccer ball.

The main conflict in the sentence is that Jamie has Joe's soccer ball. There may be additional conflicts between the two characters, but from the evidence shown in the sentence, Joe seems to be angry that Jamie has his soccer ball.

In any story, a conflict may be minor and only affect part of the story, or be the main focus of the story. An entire story may entail solving a conflict between characters. In the context of the sentence, it is not clear whether or not the entire story will revolve around Jamie taking Joe's soccer ball. However, the current conflict is based upon that information in the sentence.

Example 2

Read the following sentence and analyze how the problem can be resolved:

> Jason had homework in five subjects over the weekend, but he also had a basketball game to attend on Saturday evening.

The main problem, or conflict in the story, is that Jason has multiple obligations. He needs to complete work for school over the weekend, but he also has to, or wants to, attend a basketball game. In order to solve the problem, Jason needs to figure out how long each obligation will take. He also needs to take into account that time will be spent on daily activities, such as eating and sleeping. Once Jason figures out how much time it will take to complete homework for each subject and how much time the basketball game will take (including preparation time), he can figure out how to divide up his weekend hours. For example, Jason may say that the homework for one subject will take an hour to complete, while the homework for the other four subjects will take half an hour each. That means that Jason will need to set aside at least three hours of time to complete homework over the weekend.

Example 3

Read the following sentence from *The Call of the Wild* by Jack London and describe the main conflict in the sentence and how the conflict may be resolved:

The breaking down of discipline likewise affected the dogs in their relations with one another.

Based on the information in the sentence, an event has caused the dogs, the characters in the story, to not follow their regular routine. The sentence indicates that there has been a breaking down of discipline which is affecting how the dogs relate to each other. In order to solve this conflict, discipline needs to be restored in the story. There may be another conflict that needs to be resolved in order to re-establish discipline. However, in order to return to previous relations between the dogs, any problems that are in the way of conflict resolution need to be taken care of. The word "likewise" means also, which tells the reader that other avenues are being affected in the story besides the relations between the dogs.

Example 4

Read the following sentence and analyze the conflict between the two characters:

Mary wanted to work at the roller skating rink in the summer, but her mother wanted Mary to work in the family dental office until school started in the fall.

The two characters in the sentence have conflicting points of view. The daughter, Mary, has an opinion on where she prefers to work, while the mother has a different one. This is a familial conflict, based on whether Mary should work in the family business for the summer. The daughter is most likely torn between trying to please her family and doing what she wants to. When families have their own business, there can be a conflict of interest between children that are trying to be independent and family obligations. The mother most likely wants what is best for her daughter, but also wants what is best for the family overall. The mother may be torn between telling her daughter that she, as the person with more experience, knows what is best for the daughter versus letting her daughter figure out he\r own strengths, weaknesses, and preferences.

Setting

The setting is where a story takes place. The setting of a story may stay the same for the entire story, or change as events in the story unfold. For example, an entire story may take place in one room, or on the other end, a story could cross continents as the reader follows the characters along on a trail of events. Every story has to take place somewhere. The setting of story is described by the author in terms of what it looks like, how the character feels, and anything that is happening at that location at the time. For example, a character may be caught on a doorstep on a cold, rainy day. The character may feel frustrated as he shivers in the doorway, waiting for the heavy rain to let up a bit.

Example

When listing ways that a story set in the city has a different backdrop from a story set in the countryside, answers will vary based on current knowledge of common characteristics for each setting. A story set in a city may be different from a story set in the countryside based on the following factors:

- Number of passersby: many people on a sidewalk vs. no other people around
- Background noise: car horns vs. bird calls
- Types of surroundings: tall buildings vs. fields of corn
- Types of transportation: subways and taxis vs. horses and farm trucks

- Daily activities being carried out: sitting at a desk in a skyscraper vs. plowing fields for planting
- Type of attire: a business suit vs. dirty jeans and boots

Conclusion

The conclusion of a text is typically found in the last one or two paragraphs of the text. A conclusion wraps-up the text and reminds the reader of the main point of the text. The conclusion is the author's way of leaving the reader with a final note to remember about the paper and comes after all the supporting points of the text have been presented. For example, a paper about the importance of avoiding too much sunlight may have a conclusion that reads: By limiting sun exposure to 15 minutes a day and wearing sunscreen of at least SPF 15, a person can reduce their risk of getting skin cancer later in life.

Character trait

The traits of a character may include how they act and physical characteristics; a character trait is a behavior or physical characteristic that is unique to a specific character. For example, a character may be outgoing, which means he or she likes to talk a lot, or they may have bright red hair. These are both character traits.

An author uses character traits to describe a character in a story and help the reader to learn more about how the character acts and what they look like. By comparing the character traits in a story, the reader can see similarities and differences between characters. The author includes character traits to help the reader understand why a character may act a certain way in the story. For example, a character who is shy may not want to talk with a lot of people in a new classroom, but a character who is outgoing may want to talk with many people.

An author typically provides many details about a character so that the reader can learn more about the character's traits, motivations, relationships, and any conflicts they may have in the story. The traits of a character may include how they act and how they look. Characters are often motivated by things that have already happened in their life or how they feel about a topic. The author will often give the reader enough information about the character so that the reader can figure out why the character responds to a situation in a certain way. The author will also often give details about the relationships between characters and points they may conflict on. For example, a character may be good friends with another character; however, the two characters may disagree on where to play outside if one character likes being near the water and the other character does not.

Example

Read the following description of a character and decide, logically, whether the character is likely to go hiking outdoors:

Jeremy lived in a high-rise in Chicago. He was studious, and not very athletic. Jeremy preferred to stay indoors and read a book, rather than enjoy outdoor weather.

Based on the description of the character's traits, preferences, and personality, he is not likely to go hiking outdoors. The description indicates that the character prefers reading, rather than enjoying outdoor weather. In addition, the character lives in a tall building in the middle of a large city, in order for him to enjoy the outdoors, he would have to travel away from where he lives. The character is not likely to change his preferences. A situation may lead the character to go hiking, but

- 24 -

he is not likely to initiate the action on his own. A description of a character that is likely to go hiking outdoors may include a preference for outdoor activity and living near trails.

Character changes

Characters can change in a multitude of ways throughout a story; however, there are main aspects of a character that change. A character's identifying characteristics, such as personality or behavior traits, may change as the result of a prominent event in the story, current motivations, and conflicts. As conflicts change or are resolved, a character may no longer be motivated by striving toward a goal that was previously important to them. As the plot of a story moves along, characters can constantly change in relation to events that occur. Relationships between characters and the points of view of characters may change throughout a story as well.

Flashback, symbolism, and foreshadowing

Flashback occurs when the author of a story tells the reader events or thoughts that occurred in the past, helping the reader to make sense out of events that are currently happening in the story. Symbolism is when the author uses one object to stand for something else. For example, the author may include a flag flying high throughout a story to show pride in the characters' country and togetherness. Foreshadowing gives the reader hints that an event will occur. For example, the author may indicate that a character feels nervous and is unprepared for a competition, which can tell the reader that the character may not do well when the competition occurs. On the other hand, if the character feels confident and is well-prepared for a competition, the reader can guess that the character will do fairly well in the competition.

Points of view

An author may use first, second, or third person point of view in a text. The first person point of view is written from the perspective of a single character. Use of the pronouns 'I,' 'me,' 'we,' and 'my' indicate that the author is using first person point of view. When reading text in first person point of view, the reader sees the world through that single character's eyes. Second person point of view uses the pronoun 'you' when telling the story to another person and is the least commonly used literary point of view. Third person point of view tells a story from an all-knowing, or omniscient, perspective. The reader can get into the thoughts and points of view of multiple characters within a story when third person point of view is used.

First person point of view is told from the perspective of one person. Since this is the case, the reader gets only one side of the story, without any other angles on what may have happened in the text, such as in a personal narrative. For example, the book *The Catcher in the Rye* is told from a first person point of view, that of Holden Caulfield.

Alternately, the third person point of view gives a more objective, or whole, view of a story as it is viewed and told from many different perspectives. With this, the reader often knows what is going on in the mind of each character in the story.

Different forms of third person

When an author writes in third-person point of view, there are a few different types to choose from. The first is third person omniscient, in which there is an all knowing narrator telling the story as well as interpreting events, and relating thoughts of the characters. In third person closed or limited, the author writes in the third person, but does so from only one character's point of view.

There are two different variations of this type of narration: the narrator can either stay with the same character throughout or cycle through multiple characters over the course of the story.

Literary language and devices in biographies and autobiographies

A biography is a detailed account written about a specific person's life and their experiences. Biographies include what a person did throughout their lifetime and how those actions influenced their world and the world around them. A biography tells about the person's personality and character, whether it be good or bad. The author of a biography often studies diary entries and other personal letters to get as much valid information about the person they are writing about.

An autobiography is an account of a person's life also, but is written by the person him or herself. Autobiographies are often written because the author has experienced something bad or good that they want to tell the world about. Other times autobiographies are written to tell about a person's life from childhood to adulthood and their experiences along the way. Autobiographies can often be a mix of factual and fictional information. The author can skew the story to have a positive ending.

Figurative language

Figurative language refers to a number of ways writers deviate from literal meaning in text. Some common forms of figurative language include metaphor, simile, hyperbole, irony, and personification. A metaphor puts one idea in place of another to draw a parallel between two ideas. A simile also shows similarity between two ideas or objects, using the words like or as to draw a comparison. Note that the use of figurative language helps to describe a situation in a new way for the reader. Hyperbole is an exaggeration of an idea. Irony uses sarcasm or humor (usually with an emphasis on the opposite) to show difference from literal meaning. Personification gives life or human characteristics to an inanimate object: "The chair jumped out from underneath me" is an example of personification.

Metaphor, simile, or hyperbole

Based on current knowledge, identify whether metaphor, simile, or hyperbole is used in this sentence:

> The chiming bell was a beacon of hope for the downtrodden villagers.

Metaphor is used in this sentence to draw a parallel between "the chiming bell" and "a beacon of hope." The bell is being compared to something else in the sentence, which indicates the use of metaphor or simile, but the reader knows that the sentence does not contain a simile, because the words *like* and *as* are not used to show the comparison. The sentence also does not contain an exaggeration of facts, so the reader can conclude that hyperbole is not used. The chiming bell, as an inanimate object, does take on the quality of being a beacon of hope in the sentence, which can be use of personification in addition to displaying the use of metaphor.

Imagery

Imagery is the use of descriptive language to add life or feeling to a work of literature. Generally, it is considered to be an appeal to the senses that gives the reader a fuller appreciation for the work. The most common forms of imagery are those that appeal to the sense of sight and sound. Imagery that appeals to the sense of sight, or *visual imagery*, helps the reader picture an event in their mind, usually by including specific details in the text that are not strictly necessary for the purpose of the story, but allow the reader to more easily envision the scene. Imagery that appeals to the sense of hearing, or *auditory imagery*, most commonly appears in the form of onomatopoeia. Onomatopoeia is the use of words that phonetically imitate or suggest the sound that the word describes. An author might say, "The clock on the wall was going 'tick-tock, tick-tock.'" The words *tick* and *tock* imitate the sound that clock makes.

Summarizing and organizing information

The reader of a passage may wish to take notes to provide an overall summary of the text when they are finished. On the test, a column may be provided for "My notes about what I am reading." This allows the reader to record important facts about each paragraph for later recall. For example, for a paragraph discussing life as a young blacksmith in 18th century New England, the reader may write down "18th century blacksmith, New England." Writing a few words helps the reader to recall what each paragraph discusses. In addition to note-taking, information from a passage may be summarized and organized using the following methods:

- An outline
- A mind-map (has a central main idea, with branches of supporting details)
- A spider-map (has a main idea at the top, with supporting details branching downwards)
- A summary paragraph
- A Venn diagram or other graphic organizer (a visual method allowing the reader to see when ideas overlap)

Paraphrasing and summarizing

Paraphrasing involves stating the message in the text in the reader's own words, while keeping the original meaning of the text. Summarizing involves stating main points of the text clearly and to-the-point. Paraphrasing takes all of the original ideas and words them in a way that the reader can better understand. Summarizing takes information and states it simply, in a much shorter form. Both paraphrasing and summarizing allow the reader to remember main points explained in the text. Summarizing puts information in a short form that keeps the main points of the whole text. Paraphrasing is often done for individual ideas, while summarizing is done for an entire block of text or ideas.

Drawing a conclusion

Example 1
Draw a conclusion based on the following sentence.

New Orleans then was a mere huddle of buildings around Jackson Square; but with the purchase of the Louisiana territory from France, and the great influx of American enterprise that characterized the first quarter of the last century, development was working like yeast...

The reader needs to use prior experience and background information to draw an accurate conclusion about the sentence. The sentence describes how New Orleans grew after the "purchase of the Louisiana territory" and how "development was working like yeast". Yeast multiplies rapidly, so the reader can conclude that New Orleans was growing rapidly.

Sometimes interpreting the information in a sentence can be difficult, especially if the reader is unfamiliar with some of the words used in a sentence. Drawing a picture of what is actually happening in the sentence can help, along with looking at the words that the reader does understand in the sentence. By taking a pen or pencil and underlining important information in a

- 27 -

sentence, the reader can better understand what the author is trying to say and draw a clearer conclusion from that.

Example 2

Read the following sentence. Draw a conclusion based upon the information presented.

"A rosy-faced servant-maid opened the door, and smiled as she took the letter which he silently offered."

The reader can conclude, based on the sentence, that the servant-maid is friendly. The words "rosy-faced" and "smiled" lead the reader to this conclusion. People who are friendly are often described as having rosy complexions and smiling as a common sign of pleasantness. The reader can also assume, from the sentence, that the letter does not present any threat or unpleasantness to the servant-maid. The person presenting the letter does not have anything to say upon offering it, so perhaps he is waiting to see how the servant-maid will react.

When interpreting a sentence, always look for key words that describe a character. The author carefully crafts a description of each character, to form a picture in the reader's mind about what the character is like.

Fact and opinion

When deciding whether information is fact or opinion, a reader needs to look at whether or not the information is well-accepted by experts, in addition to being backed-up by outside sources. A fact is something that is true, regardless of what the author thinks, on the contrary, an opinion is what the author thinks, without regard to evidence to back-up that claim. For example, for a paper about caves, a fact may read: Extensive cave systems run through the soft limestone of Central Texas. An opinion may read: Caving, also called spelunking, is an enjoyable recreational activity. It is a fact that caves run throughout Central Texas, but it is the author's opinion that spelunking is an enjoyable recreational activity.

Example

Decide whether the following sentence is a fact or opinion and explain your reasoning:

The new school year will start one week before Labor Day and end on May 31st.

This sentence is a fact. The school calendar is set each year to start and finish on a certain day and while days are built into the schedule to account for bad weather, right now, the school year is set to end on May 31st. The information is factual because it is established by the school district. An opinion would express a personal feeling about the situation. For example, in the sentence, an opinion might state: The new school year should start after Labor Day and end the second week in June, so that students have the full month of August for summer.

Synthesizing a text

Synthesizing is similar to summarizing but it takes it one step further. Synthesizing involves taking the main points of a text and comparing it with existing knowledge to create a new idea, perspective, or way of thinking. Instead of using existing knowledge, synthesizing may instead be done by combining the ideas provided in two or three different texts. The reader must make connections between the texts, determine how the ideas fit together, and gather evidence to support the new perspective.

Parallelism

Parallelism means writing with a parallel structure, meaning all nouns, verbs, and phrases should have the same structure. For example, in the following sentence, the verbs are parallel: John runs fast and plays hard.

Both runs and plays are simple third person present tense verbs.

Parallelism also applies to phrases. An example of this is: My hobbies are playing the piano, running marathons, and reading books.

If the sentence was written without parallel structure for the verb phrases, the sentence would seem awkward and disjointed (i.e., My hobbies are playing the piano, running marathons and to read books).

Procedural texts

Procedural texts tell you how to accomplish a specific task. An example of this type of text is a recipe. The recipe will tell you what ingredients you need and all the information it will take to make the finished product. Another example of a procedural text is an instruction booklet that tells you how to put something together. Often procedural texts are accompanied by charts, diagrams, illustrations and graphs. These things help the reader to understand the information. Charts are used to list ingredients or parts that will be needed for the procedure. Diagrams are very helpful because they use pictures to show you how to complete a certain part of the procedure. Illustrations are helpful because they also can show you how something is supposed to look at steps along the way or a completed project. Graphs can also sometimes be used to show you information about other people's experiences with the same product or procedure.

Visual elements of a text

Visual elements—such as charts, graphs, tables, photographs, maps, and diagrams—are useful in conveying information vividly and in a summary form. Flow charts and pie charts are useful in helping readers follow a process or showing numerical information in graphic style. Tables are less stimulating but offer devices for summarizing information. Diagrams are useful and sometimes necessary in scientific writing, to explain chemical formulas, for example. Visual elements may be placed in a document close to the textual discussion or put in an appendix, labeled, and referred to in a text. Sometimes page layout makes it difficult to position visuals in optimum proximity to the corresponding text. In these cases, visuals may be placed later in the text, and readers told where they can find them. Software may be used to help the text flow around the visual for maximum impact.

Types of media presentations

Media are methods of storing or delivering information. Mass media is a type of media, such as television, radio, or the internet, that conveys information to the general public, or the masses. Print media is a type of media that includes any printed documents, such as this study material, used to transmit information. News media is a type of mass media that includes newspapers, newsletters, television news shows, and other means of transmitting news. Another widely used type is advertising media. This includes television and radio commercials, billboards, and newspaper ads. In many cases, media are used not only to convey information, but also to affect opinion and action. For instance in advertising, the advertiser conveys biased opinions about a product, hoping to profit from the recipient of the information buying the advertised product.

News media should be unbiased, but opinions can be very easily intermixed with fact, such that an undiscerning recipient may not be able to distinguish between the fact and opinion, and simply accept both as fact.

Organization of text

Authors want to have an effective text that the reader can understand. If ideas do not follow a logical order, the reader will become confused and not know what the author is trying to say. An author may organize ideas according to a timeline, cause and effect, or description of an event or setting. Without organization, the plot of a story cannot progress. Information from a text, whether it is a fictional or factual, can be organized using one of the following means:

- An outline
- A timeline
- A graphic organizer (including mind-maps, spider-maps, Venn diagrams, etc.)

A reader may take notes in the margin of a text as he or she is reading, including key points that the reader needs to remember about the text. For example, the reader may jot down the main idea of the selection, then the main idea of each supporting paragraph. If important information, such as a supporting statistic, is included in the text, the reader may jot that down in the margin as well. The reader will then take all of the information and place it in an outline, timeline, or graphic organizer. A timeline will place important facts in chronological order, whereas the other means of organization will place information in order of importance or the order it occurs in the text.

Example

Read the following paragraph from a news story and describe how the author organizes information in the story:

> The parade in honor of the town's 200th anniversary began at the corner of 57th Street at 9:00 a.m. on Saturday morning. Members of the fire department led the parade, dressed in their bright red hats and heavy yellow coats. At 9:15 a.m., members of the high school band gave a performance.

The news story uses chronological order and description to organize ideas. The reader is given information about what type of event occurred, when the event occurred, what the event was about, and who was included. The author uses adjectives such as 'bright red' and 'heavy yellow' to help the reader picture the characters in the story. By using description and chronological order, the author organizes the progression of events based upon when they occurred and what was included in each step of the story. By organizing the text, the author presents all necessary information to the reader to answer all of the following: who, what, when, where, why, and how.

Organizational Patterns

When writing, there are a variety of ways that an author can choose to organize a written work. It is important to choose the pattern that best presents the information, as not all patterns will work for every piece of writing. For example, if an author wants to write a story about a series of events that happened one week, the most logical organization for that story would be *chronological order*, or the order in which things happened. If the author were writing something informational in nature, or something intended to make an argument, they might choose instead to organize their work by *order of importance*. Order of importance can be either increasing or decreasing, depending on how the writer wants to structure the work.

Problem and Solution

Problem and solution is an organizational pattern in which the author presents some information as a problem and then discusses a solution or attempted solution to that problem. In problem and solution, there is generally one main problem, but that one problem may have several possible solutions. For example, suppose Billy wants a new video game but does not have the money. There are several possible solutions to this. He might try asking his mom to buy it for him. If that does not work, he could offer to do small jobs to earn enough money to buy it. A third possibility might be to wait until his birthday and ask for it then.

Proposition and Support

In *proposition and support*, an author will state a proposition that they believe to be true, and then provide support for that proposition in the paper. The topics that use this type of structure are generally things that reader might feel uncertain about or might not already have an opinion about. The support that the author gives for the proposition should include facts, statistics, logic, and reasoning. The more hard evidence an author can give the reader, the better it will help convince them to see things from the author's point of view.

Cause and effect

The term *cause and effect* refers to the relationship between two events that occur, where the second event occurs as a result of the first. For example, a text may discuss a school policy stating that when a student is late to school too many times, they receive a detention. Later in the text, we might see a student repeatedly arriving late to school, after which he is given a detention. In this example, the *cause* is the student being late to school, and the *effect* is the student receiving a detention.

Reading Practice Test #1

Questions 1 – 8 pertain to the following passage:

A Garden in the Desert

1. Barry lives one street up and four houses down from his best friend, Manolo. Barry, his parents, and his older brother Ricardo have lived in the small ranch house for as long as he can remember. Manolo's family moved into their house a few months before Manolo was born. At that time, 10 years ago, their housing development was only five square blocks. About 250 small, one-story houses dotted the streets. Today their housing development is three times as big, and is considered an actual neighborhood. It is called Cypress Heights.

2. There are no cypresses or any other kinds of trees in Cypress Heights. The neighborhood was built near a desert. It has no heights and no hills – just flat stretches of paved road and concrete sidewalks. Grass sprouts up between the cracks in the sidewalks, but refuses to take root on lawns. Flowers also have a hard time growing in Barry and Manolo's hot and dusty neighborhood. The only plants that grow around most of the houses are patches of ragged-looking weeds.

3. In contrast to the dusty lawns, most of the ranch houses are very well kept. The outsides of the houses are freshly painted, and many lawns are decorated with bird baths and patio furniture. The lack of gardens and lawns, however, makes the neighborhood look dusty, downtrodden, and old. Without grass roots to knit a protective net in the soil, the wind picks up dirt and blows it all over the roads, roofs, and sidewalks. After a windy day, everything in Cypress Heights is covered in brown and gray dust.

4. Manolo and Barry love living in Cypress Heights because their houses are so close, and each boy can easily get to the other's house. A short fence surrounds Manolo's backyard. Manolo can jump over the fence and walk along the path in the neighbor's backyard to Barry's street. From there, Manolo can walk past three houses to get to Barry's. The fence around Barry's backyard is too high to jump over and too smooth to climb, so Barry has to stick to the streets to get to Manolo's house.

5. One summer day, Barry rode his bike over to Manolo's house. He brought a backpack with a picnic lunch.

6. "Let's go to the playground at the school," said Barry. "I have two peanut butter and jelly sandwiches and two juice boxes for lunch. We can stay there all afternoon."

"Sounds good," said Manolo. His older sister was watching him while his mother was at work. He asked his sister, Rosa, for permission.

"Just be back before five o'clock," said Rosa. "Mom should be home by then."

7. Barry and Manolo's school was about a mile away. It was a long, brown, one-story building with big windows and a large play set in the front. In the back were two sets of train tracks. Usually, the trains only ran at night, but every so often a freight train would pass the school during the day, making the windows rattle and the children rush from their seats to watch it.

8. On their way to the schoolyard, they passed a house that had just been sold a few weeks earlier. On the yard, instead of dusty weeds, was white gravel. Dotted around the lawn were different cactus plants. Barry and Manolo stopped their bikes and stared at the lawn.

9. "It looks great," said Barry. "But I don't want cactus plants in my yard. What if I ran into one while playing tag? That would hurt!"

"There are other plants that work in this area," said a voice from behind a large cactus.

10. A woman with short brown hair stepped out from behind the cactus and walked over to Barry and Manolo. She had a wide-brimmed hat on her head.

"We planted cacti because they don't need much water," said the woman with a smile. She waved her hand toward her house. "It is too expensive to water plants or a lawn. But there are other drought-resistant plants that will do well here."

11. "What kind of plant is 'drought resistant'?" asked Manolo.

"Basically, it is a plant that doesn't need much water," said the woman. "They include plants like lavender, aloe, lamb's ear, and oriental yew. I have some of those in pots ready to be planted. If you promise to take care of them, I can give you some to plant in your yards."

12. "Sure!" said Barry and Manolo at once.

The woman motioned to the boys to follow her behind her house. She put several small plants in a low, flat box attached to the back of her bicycle. She strapped down the plants and climbed on the seat.

"Lead the way," she said.

"Thank you," said Barry. "By the way, I'm Barry and this is Manolo."

"I'm Mrs. Juarez," said the woman. "Nice to meet you."

13. "Wait a minute," said Barry. "You just moved in. Shouldn't we give presents to you?"

"That's okay," laughed Mrs. Juarez. "I don't have any more room in my garden, so you are doing me a favor by taking them. But, I will take cookies if you have them!"

"Sounds good," said Barry. The three of them headed towards the boys' houses, ready to break ground on their new gardens.

1. What is the main objective of paragraphs 2 and 3?

    a. To describe Manolo's house
    b. To describe Barry's house
    c. To describe Manolo's and Barry's friendship
    d. To describe Manolo's and Barry's neighborhood

2. Which sentence in paragraph 3 showed that Cypress Heights residents care about how their houses look?

    a. "The outsides of the houses are freshly painted, and many lawns are decorated with bird baths and patio furniture"
    b. "The lack of gardens and lawns, however, makes the neighborhood look dusty, downtrodden, and old"
    c. "Without grass roots to knit a protective net in the soil, the wind picks up dirt and blows it all over the roads, roofs, and sidewalks"
    d. "After a windy day, everything in Cypress Heights is covered in brown and gray dust"

3. Why do Barry and Manolo like living close to each other?

    a. Because it is convenient for them to visit each other
    b. Because Barry's fence is too high to climb
    c. Because their bikes don't work
    d. Because Manolo has a shorter walk

4. Who did the boys meet on their way to the schoolyard?

    a. Barry's parents
    b. Mrs. Juarez
    c. Rosa, Manolo's sister
    d. Manolo's mother

5. What are "drought-resistant" plants?

    a. Plants that can live in very hot climates
    b. Plants that can live in very cold climates
    c. Plants that can live in very dry climates
    d. Plants that can live in very wet climates

6. Instead of grass, what did Mrs. Juarez put on her lawn to keep dust and dirt from blowing around?

    a. Lavender
    b. Yucca
    c. Aloe
    d. Gravel

7. What did Barry mean when he said, "You just moved in. Shouldn't we give presents to you?"

    a. Mrs. Juarez was too busy to give presents
    b. Traditionally, new neighbors receive gifts, not give them
    c. Mrs. Juarez doesn't know Barry and Manolo well enough to know what they want
    d. Barry and Manolo shouldn't take gifts from strangers

8. What phrase best sums up the lesson Mrs. Juarez taught Manolo and Barry?

    a. Good friends turn up in unlikely places
    b. Cookies will help you make friends
    c. With the right plants, gardens can grow anywhere
    d. With the right tools, gardens can grow anywhere

Questions 9 – 11 pertain to the following letter:

Thomas's First Complaint Letter

> February 24, 2011
> Thomas Goodwill
> 1234 Main Street
> Thompson, Texas 77482

Romco Toys

8765 Madison Avenue

New York, New York 10008

To the customer service department:

I bought a Romco talking wind-up doll for my little sister from your website on November 12, 2010. The doll arrived on November 20. My sister opened the box on Christmas Day, and the doll worked fine until three days ago. At that time, my sister noticed that the winding part was getting harder to twist. Now it will not twist at all. The doll no longer talks.

My mom noticed that the papers that came with the doll state that it is guaranteed to work for one year. The papers also state that if the doll stopped working within a year, we should send it back to your company for a replacement. The doll is enclosed in this box. We would like a new doll to replace this defective one.

Thank you for your time. My sister looks forward to getting a new doll that works.

Sincerely,

Thomas Goodwill

9. Why did Thomas write this letter?

    a. To invite a friend over for Christmas
    b. To replace a doll he bought that broke
    c. To buy a wind-up talking doll
    d. To ask about a wind-up talking doll

10. How long is the guarantee for the doll?

    a. One year
    b. One month
    c. Two years
    d. Three months

11. What does the word "defective" mean?
    a. Ugly
    b. Definitive
    c. Broken
    d. Expensive

Questions 12 – 15 pertain to both Thomas's letter and Romco Toy's reply letter:

Romco's Toys Reply Letter

March 5, 2011
Customer Service Department
Romco Toys
8765 Madison Avenue
New York, New York 10008

Dear Customer:

Romco's wind-up doll was a very popular item with girls this Christmas. Unfortunately, many of the toys sold before the holidays had a defective winding mechanism that gradually became harder to turn. It made it impossible to operate the doll's unique speaking features. This defect is the responsibility of the manufacturers, so we are asking our customers to help the company recoup some of the loss it experienced due to this problem.

Included in this letter is a form we are asking all customers to fill out to receive a replacement doll. The form provides Romco with the documentation necessary to recover money lost from replacing the defective dolls. Please fill out the form and put it in the prepaid envelope provided. Romco will assume all postage costs for the letter and the replacement doll. After the form is received, Romco will send a new doll free of charge. Thank you for your concern in this matter.

Sincerely,

Romco Customer Service Department

12. According to both letters, what is the correct format for writing the name of a town and state in an address?
    a. anywhere Texas
    b. anywhere, Texas
    c. Anywhere Texas
    d. Anywhere, Texas

13. Why did Romco Toys call Thomas "Customer" in its letter?
    a. Romco Toys had so many complaints it couldn't write individual letters
    b. Thomas did not write his name in his letter
    c. In the letter, Romco Toys said it is standard procedure to not use customers' names
    d. Thomas was not a customer; his sister received the doll

14. How long did it take Romco Toys to reply to Thomas's letter?
    a. Two weeks
    b. Two months
    c. Nine weeks
    d. Nine days

15. Tone in writing describes the feelings or impressions a piece of writing give the reader. Just a few examples of tone are happy, sad, polite, and angry. Which of the following best describes the tone of both letters?
    a. Angry
    b. Polite
    c. Silly
    d. Rude

Questions 16 – 25 pertain to the following passage:

Hobie's Journey across the Finish Line

1. "On your marks, get set, GO!"

While the crack of the starting gun was still ringing in his ears, Hobie straightened his right leg so fast he felt a twinge in his knee. He then swung his left leg straight in front of him. When he looked up, he was surprised to find himself nearly halfway up the track. His heart was thumping hard and fast in his chest.

2. "Go easy," Hobie thought. "You have three-and-a-half more laps to go."

He took a deep breath and lifted his legs slightly to relax his stride. His shoulders dropped a little as he swung his arms. Hobie's chest felt a little less tight. His feet tapped the track as Hobie matched the sound of his footfalls to those of the runners behind him.

"Try to save some steam for the end," said Coach Bennett. "That's when you can catch up to the jack rabbits that used up everything in the first lap."

3. Hobie loved going fast for as long as he could remember. In kindergarten, he was always first to cross the finish line during running races at recess. He won an award in second grade for running the fastest mile in gym. But every spring, Hobie chose playing baseball over track, despite his parent's pleas to consider track.

4. "You're such a good runner," said his mother. "And it would be so much easier because we would only have to drive to one practice."

Hobie's older brother, Martin, was a member of the county's local track club. Martin had joined seven years earlier and was now one of the team's star sprinters. But Hobie did not want to be compared to his brother on the track. Few people in the town's Little League association even knew that Hobie had a brother, much less a brother who could run 100 meters in less than 15 seconds. Hobie wasn't the strongest player on his baseball team. He didn't like spending so much time on the bench, but he loved how he was always called "Hobie" or "Hobie Smith," never "Martin's little brother."

- 37 -

5. Three months ago, in March, Hobie was all set for his fifth year in Little League. He had been practicing throwing and batting after school. His aim was improving, and so was his throwing speed. Hobie hoped his efforts would mean he would spend more time in his position, right outfield, and less time on the bench. Then Hobie and Martin's father had an accident at work. Mr. Smith fell from a ladder and broke his leg and arm. He could not work or drive for six months.

6. "I don't have time to get home from work and drive to two different practices," said Hobie's mother, Mrs. Smith, to Hobie. "And it's not fair to make Martin switch to baseball after he's been in track for seven years and is doing so well. I'm sorry Hobie, but you have only one choice for a sport this spring, and it's track. You don't have to join, but if you don't, you're staying home with Dad."

7. Luckily, the coach for Hobie's track team, Coach Bennett, was new. He didn't know Hobie even had a brother. Also, Hobie turned out to be better at long distances. Coach Bennett had him focus on the mile and the 800-meters events. At the last meet, Hobie ran a mile in just under seven minutes.

"You keep that up, and I'm kidnapping you for the high school cross-country running team in the fall!" Coach Bennett joked after the race.

8. Hobie was now finishing his first turn with only two other runners ahead of him. He couldn't believe how well he had done this season. In baseball, Hobie always struggled to pay attention in the field. He loved batting, running bases, and catching fly balls, but hated the endless hours of waiting out in the field or on the bench for something to happen. In track, he was always moving. And, for the first time, he was doing very well. He was the fastest distance runner on his team, and had won three out of the seven races he ran that season. Hobie pushed his legs a bit faster and caught up to the second-place runner. There was just one person blocking his view of the finish line.

9. Hobie felt his legs fly through the air and his chest start to hurt a little. He puffed his cheeks and swung his arms hard. Two more laps to go. Hobie kept pace a few feet behind the runner in the lead until they rounded the last bend of the track. Hobie drew a deep, ragged breath and started to run a little faster, making the distance between him and the other runner a few feet shorter. Hobie kept sprinting until he was running side by side with the runner in the lead. The finish line came into view. With his last ounce of strength, Hobie pushed past the other runner and swung his arms as hard as he could, flying over the finish line four yards ahead of the other runner.

10. "Good job!" shouted Coach Bennett, rushing out to jog alongside him. Hobie slowed down and leaned over to catch his breath, placing his hands on his knees. Then he looked up into the stands and saw his father waving his good arm. Hobie waved back. He was no longer angry that he couldn't play baseball. He was glad to be running track.

16. Why did Hobie choose baseball instead of track?

    a. Hobie's parents wanted him to play baseball
    b. Hobie wanted to avoid being compared to his older brother
    c. Hobie was a better baseball player than runner
    d. Hobie's brother, Martin, also played baseball

17. In paragraph 1, what does the word "twinge" mean?

    a. Hurt
    b. Bend
    c. Break
    d. Loosen

18. Which sentence from paragraphs 3 and 4 shows that Hobie is a good runner?

    a. "Hobie wasn't the strongest player on his baseball team"
    b. "Hobie loved going fast for as long as he could remember"
    c. "But Hobie did not want to be compared to his brother on the track"
    d. "In kindergarten, he was always first to cross the finish line during running races at recess"

19. Why did Hobie switch to track instead of playing baseball for the fifth year in a row?

    a. The new track coach, Coach Bennett, didn't know Hobie's brother
    b. Hobie did not make the baseball team
    c. Hobie's father was no longer able to drive him to practice
    d. Hobie broke his arm falling off a ladder

20.

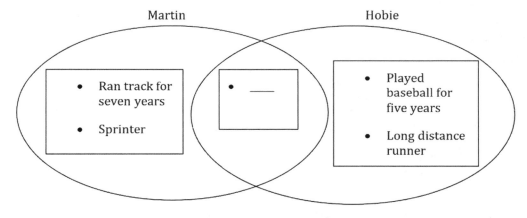

Which of the following phrases belongs in the blank?

    a. Good at running
    b. Older brother
    c. Younger brother
    d. Ran on high school cross-country team

21. What is the most likely lesson a reader will learn from this story?

    a. Track is a better sport than baseball
    b. It is dangerous to use ladders
    c. Hard decisions can have positive outcomes
    d. Big brothers like to be compared to little brothers

- 39 -

22. Increased tension or excitement in a story is called suspense. How does the author build suspense in the story "Hobie's Journey across the Finish Line"?

    a. By describing how Hobie's father hurt himself at work

    b. By describing how Hobie got better at running long distances

    c. By showing why Hobie had to switch to track from baseball

    d. By describing how Hobie got from third to first place in the race

23. Which choice is the best summary of this story?

    a. Despite showing a talent for running, Hobie chose to play baseball to avoid comparisons to his older brother. His father's accident forced him to join track, where he did well

    b. Hobie disliked his older brother and decided to get back at him by joining baseball instead of track. Hobie later joined track to show his brother, Martin, that he is a better runner

    c. Hobie wasn't very good at baseball, so he practiced throwing, catching, and hitting every day after school until he got better

    d. A boy loved to run, but chose to play baseball instead. Later, he switched to track

24. What is the best definition of the word "ragged" as it is used in paragraph 9?

    a. Roughly kept

    b. Having a torn edge or outline

    c. Worn-out from stress and strain

    d. Wearing tattered clothes

25. Based on the events of this story, what is Hobie most likely to do next year?

    a. Join track as a sprinter to compete against his brother

    b. Join Little League and compete to be a pitcher

    c. Join track as a long distance runner

    d. Join Little League and play right field

Questions 26 – 30 pertain to the following passage:

Sticky Water

1. News flash: water is sticky.

This is a surprise to many people because water does not seem sticky. In fact, it's the first thing that people reach for to wash away stickiness and any other kind of dirt. The second item, of course, is soap.

2. Water and things like glue are sticky in different ways. Glue is sticky in two ways. Water is sticky in only one way. Glue feels and acts sticky. It is used to join objects such as paper, wood, and plastic together. Water does not feel or act sticky.

3. Glue is sticky in two ways. One way is called adhesion. This is when glue, after it is poured on a surface, spreads into tiny holes and dents and hardens. The glue holds the surfaces together like the pieces of a jigsaw puzzle. But for glue to work well, it also needs to stick to itself and hold together. This is called cohesion.

4. Water does not have adhesion. If you pour it on a piece of wood, the wood will absorb the water, but water will not harden to make two things stick together. Water does have cohesion. Water is a unique substance made up of two elements: hydrogen (H) and oxygen (O). Water is made up of two parts hydrogen and one part oxygen. The formula for water is

- 40 -

H2O. The hydrogen atoms not only stick to the oxygen, but also to other water molecules, much in the same way magnets stick to metal. Water molecules stick to each other because of "hydrogen bonds." If water did not hold together, it could not be a liquid. It would boil and turn into steam.

5. To see the "stickiness" of water, try the following experiment. This experiment is not dangerous, and it only requires ordinary objects that you probably have at home. However, you will end up spilling some water, so ask an adult if it is okay to do the experiment before starting.

Sticky Water Experiment

6. You will need the following for this experiment:

One short plastic cup (the kind adults use at parties for punch works very well)

One small pitcher of water

At least 20 pennies

A sponge or rag for spills

7. First, fill the plastic cup with water from the pitcher. Make sure you fill the cup all the way up to the rim. Don't spill any water! If you spill water, wipe it up. Make sure the very full glass is sitting on a dry spot.

8. Next, carefully slip a penny into the cup and look closely. Did any of the water spill over the edge? Probably not. Continue adding pennies slowly to avoid splashing. Slip them in gently. Do not throw them in.

9. Keep putting in pennies until water spills over the edge. How many pennies did it take for the water to spill over? It was probably more than you thought. Most people who do this experiment think one or two pennies will make the very full glass spill, but usually it takes more than 10 pennies. The explanation for this is cohesion. Each time you put in a penny, the water molecules hold on tighter and tighter to each other. Finally, when there is absolutely no more room in the glass and they're hanging over the edge of the glass, the water spills. One time, a scientist was able to get 25 pennies into the glass before it spilled! Now that's sticky water!

26. Why did the author start this article with the words "News flash"?
    a. To show it is a news article
    b. The author made a mistake.
    c. To attract readers' attention
    d. Because it is a news story

27. Which of these phrases belongs in the blank line in the chart?

Different Kinds of Stickiness

Adhesion	Cohesion
Sticks to surfaces	Sticks to other molecules in the liquid
Fills in holes	Holds the liquid together
Hardens	Does not harden
Acts like a jigsaw puzzle	_____

    a. Does not spill
    b. Acts like a magnet on metal
    c. Acts like water in a cup
    d. Boils and turns into steam

28. Why is it important that the cup is sitting on a dry spot?
    a. To keep adults from getting upset about the mess
    b. To make the experiment safe and clean
    c. To keep the pennies dry before they go in the water
    d. To make it clear when the water spills from too many pennies

29. Why did the author call water sticky?
    a. Because of the way the water molecules are attracted to each other
    b. Because of the way water sticks to surfaces
    c. Because of the way water feels on our hands
    d. Because we use water to wash up sticky messes

30. Which of the following choices is the best example of how water is sticky?
    a. The force of gravity makes rivers and streams flow downhill
    b. Water combined with soap is useful for cleaning
    c. A paper clip can float because of the surface tension of water
    d. Too much water in a cup will spill over the edge

Questions 31 – 33 pertain to the following passage:

Water and Keeping It Clean

    1. We take water for granted. It is all around us in lakes, streams, pools, and oceans. We only need to turn on the tap to get some to drink or turn on the shower to wash ourselves with it.

- 42 -

Water is everywhere. Most of the time we welcome having water, except when it floods into our basements or onto our floors.

2. It's important to remember that water is a valuable and life-sustaining substance. Without water, humans and most animals and plants would die within a few days. Water is also unique. It is the only natural substance that can be in three states – liquid, solid (ice), and gas (steam). For water to change from one state to another, it has to change temperature. To stay in a liquid state, water must be between 33°F and 211°F. Water freezes, or turns into ice, at 32°F. It boils, or turns into steam, at 212°F.

3. The freezing point for water does not change, but the boiling point for water changes depending on how high you are above sea level. The higher up you go, the lower the boiling point. So, water that will boil at 212°F by the ocean will only need to be 186.4°F to boil at 14,000 feet. That's good to know on your next hike up the Rocky Mountains!

4. Here is another fun fact about water. When it is in its solid form, ice, it is less dense. Ice, which is strong enough to hold up a full-sized truck on a frozen lake, is lighter than water. That is why ice floats.

5. Despite its unique qualities and its importance to our survival, water is almost constantly under attack, and the enemy is pollution. There are many things that pollute water, including chemicals in fertilizers that can be washed off fields and into streams when it rains. The waste we flush from our houses has pollutants. Most of it is treated at wastewater treatment plants, but a tiny amount still leaks back into lakes, rivers, and oceans.

6. The good news is that many farmers are changing the way they take care of their crops to prevent chemicals from washing into rivers. Scientists and engineers are working with wastewater treatment plants to make them better at keeping all pollutants out of lakes and oceans.

7. Even ordinary people can help keep water clean. Picking up trash helps keep it from blowing into nearby water sources. It is especially important to pick up plastic because plastic does not break down like paper and wood. Fish and other animals in the water get tangled in plastic bags. They may also mistake plastic objects for food, eat them, and die.

8. So, next time you are out for a walk or at a park, be sure to pick up trash and make sure it ends up in a garbage can. You will not only make the place look better, but you will also be saving the lives of animals in the water and keeping the water clean.

31. What does the phrase "take water for granted" in paragraph 1 mean?
   a. To take water around for drinking
   b. To notice that water is everywhere, in lakes and in oceans
   c. To welcome water, except when it floods our houses
   d. To not value it, and to expect it to always be around

32. What is the boiling point of water at 14,000 feet above sea level?
   a. 330.2°F
   b. 211°F
   c. 186.4°F
   d. 212°F

33. Which one of these statements is a fact?

    a. There should be a stricter law against people who pollute the water
    b. Water pollution isn't the biggest problem facing the world today
    c. People who pollute the water are bad
    d. Fertilizers washed off of fields by rain pollute nearby streams, rivers, and lakes

Questions 34 – 36 pertain to both articles "Sticky Water" and "Water and Keeping it Clean":

34. What is one idea expressed in both articles?

    a. Water is a unique substance
    b. All living creatures need water to survive
    c. Water is wet
    d. Water is sticky

35. How is the article "Sticky Water" different from "Water and Keeping It Clean"?

    a. "Sticky Water" shows where water comes from and "Water and Keeping It Clean" talks about water pollution
    b. "Sticky Water" mostly describes a property of water and "Water and Keeping It Clean" mostly talks about a problem related to water
    c. "Sticky Water" is about cohesion and "Water and Keeping It Clean" is about adhesion
    d. "Sticky Water" is a true story and "Water and Keeping It Clean" is made up

36. In what kind of book or magazine would these articles most likely be found?

    a. English language arts
    b. Social studies
    c. Math
    d. Science

Questions 37-38 pertain to the following poem.

"Thinking" by Walter D. Wintle

> If you think you are beaten, you are;
> If you think you dare not, you don't.
> If you'd like to win, but you think you can't,
> It is almost a cinch you won't.
>
> If you think you'll lose, you've lost;
> For out in this world we find
> Success begins with a person's will
> It's all in the state of mind.
>
> If you think you're outclassed, you are;
> You've got to think high to rise.
> You've got to be sure of yourself before
> You can ever win the prize.
>
> Life's battles don't always go
> To the stronger or faster man;
> But sooner or later the person who wins
> Is the one who thinks he can!

37. What type of literary device is used in stanzas 1 and 3 to emphasize the author's point?

   a. comparing and contrasting
   b. repetition for emphasis
   c. exaggeration or hyperbole
   d. personification

38. What is the main idea of this poem?

   a. If you perform well, you can succeed in life.
   b. If you have a strong enough will, you can do anything.
   c. If you think you cannot do something, then it often becomes true.
   d. It's better to be smart than athletic.

Answer Key and Explanations for Test #1

TEKS Standard §110.7(10)(A) and (D) and (9)(D)(i)

1. D: The main objective of these paragraphs is to describe Manolo's and Barry's neighborhood.

TEKS Standard §110.7(7)(C)

2. A: The first sentence shows that Cypress Heights residents do everything in their control (painting their houses and decorating their lawns) to make their places look nice.

TEKS Standard §110.7(7)(C) and (8)(D)

3. A: Barry and Manolo like living close to each other because it makes it convenient for them to visit each other.

TEKS Standard §110.7(7)(C), (8)(B), and (8)(C)

4. B: The boys met Mrs. Juarez, who had just moved in.

TEKS Standard §110.7(3)(A) and (B)

5. C: Plants that can live in very dry climates are called drought-resistant.

TEKS Standard §110.7(7)(C)

6. D: Mrs. Juarez put gravel on her lawn instead of grass. She used gravel because she wouldn't have to water it.

TEKS Standard §110.7(6)(F)

7. B: Traditionally, new neighbors receive gifts, not give them. That is why Barry asked Mrs. Juarez that question.

TEKS Standard §110.7(7)(D) and (9)(D)(i)

8. C: While Mrs. Juarez may turn out to be a good friend, the main lesson she taught Barry and Manolo is that with the right plants, gardens can grow anywhere.

TEKS Standard §110.7(6)(F), (7)(D) and (9)(D)(i)

9. B: Thomas wanted to replace a doll he bought for his sister, which broke before the warranty was up.

TEKS Standard §110.7(7)(C)

10. A: The warranty or guarantee for the doll was for one year.

TEKS Standard §110.7(3)(B) and (C)

11. C: The word "defective" is another way of saying "broken."

TEKS Standard §110.7(6)(H) and (7)(C)

12. D: The correct form for writing the name of a town and state is Anywhere, Texas.

TEKS Standard §110.7(6)(F)

13. A: Romco did not have time to write an individual letter to all of the customers with complaints, so they wrote a general letter to all people who complained.

TEKS Standard §110.7(7)(C) and (9)(D)(i)

14. D: It took nine days for Romco to reply to Thomas's letter according to the dates on the letters.

TEKS Standard §110.7(9)(A) and (10)(E)

15. B: The tone in both letters is polite.

TEKS Standard §110.7(7)(C) and (8)(C)

16. B: Hobie chose baseball because his brother was already running track and he didn't want to be compared to him.

TEKS Standard §110.7(3)(B)

17. A: Twinge also means to hurt. Hobie flexed his leg so fast that it made his knee hurt a little.

TEKS Standard §110.7(7)(C)

18. D: Always being the first one to cross the finish line is a good indication that Hobie was (and still is) a good runner.

TEKS Standard §110.7(7)(C) and (8)(C)

19. C: After suffering an accident at work, Hobie's father couldn't drive him to practice. Hobie's mother gave him a choice: run track with his brother or stay home with his dad.

TEKS Standard §110.7(6)(F), (7)(C), (9)(D)(ii), and (10)(C)

20. A: While Martin and Hobie may be different in many ways, they are both good at running.

TEKS Standard §110.7(6)(E) and (9)(D)(i)

21. C: Hobie had a hard decision to make. Forced to give up baseball, he had to choose between playing a sport where he might be compared to his brother or staying at home. Hobie found out that difficult decisions sometimes turn out all right in the end.

TEKS Standard §110.7(6)(F) and (8)(C)

22. D: The author's step-by-step account of how Hobie made it from third to first place in the race increased the tension or suspense in the story.

TEKS Standard §110.7(10)(A), (7)(D), and (9)(D)(i)

23. A: This summary includes all the important information in the story, and is accurate.

TEKS Standard §110.7(3)(B)

24. C: Hobie's breathing became ragged because he was worn out from running so fast for so long.

TEKS Standard §110.7(6)(H)

25. C: Hobie is most likely to rejoin track the following year as a long-distance runner, an area where he showed talent. It will also allow him to avoid comparisons to his brother, who is a sprinter.

TEKS Standard §110.7(10)(A)

26. C: The author started the story with the phrase "News flash" to attract the readers' attention. The article is about a scientific fact. It is not a breaking news story.

TEKS Standard §110.7(6)(F) and (9)(D)(ii)

27. B: Cohesion is a kind of stickiness in which molecules stick to each other via attraction, much in the same way a magnet sticks to metal.

TEKS Standard §110.7(7)(C)

28. D: The point of the experiment is to see how many pennies it takes for an already full glass of water to overflow. That is why the glass must be in a clean, dry place.

TEKS Standard §110.7(10)(A) and (7)(C)

29. A: Water is sticky because its molecules stick to each other.

TEKS Standard §110.7(6)(H) and (7)(D)

30. C: A paper clip can float on top of water because the molecules are stuck together and can hold it up.

TEKS Standard §110.7(3)(B)

31. D: To take for granted means to not value something and to assume it will always be there.

TEKS Standard §110.7(7)(C)

32. C: 186.4°F is the boiling point of water at 14,000 feet.

TEKS Standard §110.7(6)(F) and (7)(C)

33. D: This sentence is a proven fact. The other three statements are opinions.

TEKS Standard §110.7(8)(A) and (9)(D)(i)

34. A: Both articles note that water is a unique substance.

TEKS Standard §110.7(7)(C)

35. B: The first article talks about a property of water (its stickiness) and the second article talks about a problem related to water (pollution).

- 48 -

TEKS Standard §110.7(6)(E) and (6)(H)

36. D: Articles about the properties of water are most likely to be found in a science text.

TEKS Standard §110.7(9)(B)

37. B: The author uses repeated language throughout stanzas 1 and 3, such as "if you," which is said three times in stanza 1, and "you've got," in stanza 3 to emphasize his point through repetition. Repetition is also used in the meaning of the lines, as lines 1, 2, and 3 mean essentially the same thing. The same meaningful repetition is found in the third stanza, where the author uses different words with the same meaning to drive his point in.

TEKS Standard §110.7(8)(A)

38. C: The main idea of this poem is that a person's thoughts influence their success. This poem describes an effect called "self-fulfilling prophecy," where a person does not think they can achieve something, so they do not try or do not give it their best effort, and do not succeed because they didn't think they could.

Reading Practice Test #2

Questions 1 – 9 pertain to the following passage:

War: The Card Game

1. Rain came down in sheets, drumming on the windows and then splashing on the tiny deck that stuck out from Mona and Yuri's third floor apartment. Mona looked out at the yard outside the apartment complex. Large puddles were forming in the middle of the lawn, making a small lake around a tree where she, her brother Yuri, and the neighborhood children liked to play.

2. "I am so sick of this rain," said Mona. It was Saturday. Her mother, a nurse, was sleeping after working overnight at the hospital. Mona and her brother usually went outside to let her mother sleep, but the rain was so heavy that even with raincoats and hoods, they'd be drenched in minutes. They watched cartoons for a couple of hours, but soon grew restless. It was 11 a.m., too early to eat the lunch their mother had left them. It was also too early for their mother to wake up. She went to bed around 7 a.m. and didn't like to get up before 3 in the afternoon.

3. "Let's play War," said Yuri.

"War?" asked Mona. "Are you out of your mind? Mom is asleep. Running around the apartment and whooping it up will wake her in no time. You know how grumpy she gets when we wake her early."

"This is a different kind of game," said Yuri. "My friend Peter taught it to me at the babysitter's yesterday afternoon. You play it with cards."

4. "Cards?" said Mona. "How do you play War with cards?"

"Like this," said Yuri. He took a deck of playing cards from the dining room cabinet. "First you shuffle them. I'm not very good at that."

5. After Mona shuffled the cards Yuri dealt half the deck to Mona and half to himself. Then he put his cards face down in a pile in front of him and told Mona to do the same. He put his hand over the pile and told Mona to take the first card from the top of her pile and lay it down between them on the count of three.

"One, two, three!" counted Mona and Yuri. Mona had a five and Yuri's card was a six.

- 50 -

6. "The higher card wins, so I take this round," said Yuri, picking up both cards and setting them next to where he was sitting. Yuri explained that in the card game War, both players put down a card at the same time and the player with the higher valued card takes both cards. He explained that aces are the highest valued cards, followed by kings, queens, and jacks. Then the cards go by their numbers—10, 9, 8, and so on.

7. "What if both players have the same number?" asked Mona.

"That's when you have a war!" said Yuri excitedly. "If you both have the same number, you each put down two more cards face down and then turn the third card up. Whoever has the higher card then takes all eight cards. We play until we run out of cards and the player with the most cards wins. Isn't it easy?"

8. "Yes," said Mona.

Mona and Yuri continued playing until both of them put down a jack.

"War!" they whispered excitedly.

They put down two cards and then a third card that they placed face up. Mona had a queen and Yuri had a six. Mona took all eight cards. At the end of the game Mona had 30 cards and Yuri had 22.

9. "I won!" said Mona excitedly.

"Beginner's luck," said Yuri.

"Actually, this game is all luck," said Mona.

"True," said Yuri. "Want to go best out of three?"

"You bet!" said Mona.

10. They played for the rest of the morning, until it was time to eat lunch. In what seemed like no time at all, their mother was awake and they were planning a quick trip out of the house.

"That was a great game," said Mona. "Thanks for teaching me, Yuri."

1. What does the writer mean by the phrase "rain came down in sheets"?
    a. It was raining on the laundry
    b. It was raining very hard
    c. It was raining lightly
    d. It was raining diagonally

2. Why couldn't Mona and Yuri run around the apartment and make noise?
    a. The downstairs neighbor would be angry
    b. There were strict rules against making noise before noon on weekends
    c. Mona was sick and couldn't stand loud noises
    d. Mona and Yuri's mother was asleep

3. What time was Yuri's and Mona's mother expected to wake up?

    a. 7 a.m.
    b. 11 a.m.
    c. 3 p.m.
    d. 5 p.m.

4. What kind of game did Yuri suggest playing?

    a. A card game
    b. A computer game
    c. A board game
    d. A running game

5. Which card has the highest value in War?

    a. Ace
    b. Queen
    c. King
    d. Jack

6. What has to happen in the game to have a "war"?

    a. One player must have an ace
    b. Both players must have the same card
    c. Both players must run out of cards
    d. One player must have a king

7. Who won the first game?

    a. Yuri
    b. Mona and Yuri's mother
    c. Mona
    d. Yuri and Mona tied.

8. What did Mona mean when she said "Actually, this game is all luck."?

    a. The game does not require any skill to win
    b. The game requires a lot of skill to win
    c. Only lucky people win the game
    d. A person needs lucky numbers to win

9. Mona and Yuri are playing War. Mona puts down a king and Yuri puts down a jack. Who wins the round?

    a. Mona
    b. Yuri
    c. Nobody, because it's a tie
    d. Nobody, because kings aren't allowed in the game

Questions 10 – 12 pertain to the following passage:

Ann Richards: The First Woman Governor of Texas

1. Born Dorothy Ann Willis in 1933, Gov. Ann Richards did not start out in politics. She taught social studies and history at Fulmore Junior High School in Austin. Then, she got married and stopped teaching to raise her family. While at home, Gov. Richards volunteered for political campaigns and causes. She worked especially hard to make sure people were treated and paid fairly.

2. In 1976, Gov. Richards successfully campaigned for the position of Travis County Commissioner. Six years later, she was elected Texas State Treasurer. She was the first woman in 50 years to be elected to a statewide office in Texas. She stayed in that office until 1990, when she was elected governor of Texas.

3. As governor, Gov. Richards worked hard to make the state government work better. She asked that the records and budgets of every state agency be looked at carefully, a process called an audit. She changed the way decisions were made for schools by giving parents and teachers living and working in the district more power to make important decisions. She also worked to make Texas safer by opposing, or speaking out against, dangerous guns called assault weapons. She arranged for more education programs at prisons so that prisoners would have more chances to improve themselves.

4. Gov. Richards appointed women and minorities to state government positions to increase opportunities within the state government for many different kinds of people. Gov. Richards served one term as governor. She lost in 1994 to George W. Bush, who later became president of the United States.

5. Gov. Richards was famous for having a great sense of humor and not being afraid to make fun of herself. She once joked about her hair being heavily styled by saying, "Neither snow nor rain can move my hair." To show that women were just as capable as men, she once said about a famous dancing couple, "Ginger Rogers did everything that Fred Astaire did. She just did it backwards and in high heels." Gov. Richards kept working to make peoples' lives better, even after she left politics.

10. What did Ann Richards do before she entered politics?

   a. Campaigned for the Travis County commissioner position
   b. Became governor of Texas
   c. Taught social studies and history
   d. Audited Texas state agencies

11. What is paragraph 3 mostly about?

   a. Gov. Richards's humor
   b. Gov. Richards's life before politics
   c. Gov. Richards's first job in politics
   d. Gov. Richards's achievements as governor

12. What did Richards mean when she said, "Neither snow nor rain will move my hair."?

   a. Her hairstyle was very stiff and strong
   b. Her hair was very important to her
   c. She used to work in the post office
   d. She needed strong hair to be governor of Texas

Questions 13 – 16 pertain to the following passage:

Kay Bailey Hutchinson: The First Woman Senator of Texas

1. Kay Bailey Hutchinson was born and raised in Texas. She went to the University of Texas and graduated with a law degree in 1967. One of her first jobs was as a news reporter for a TV station. In 1972, Sen. Hutchinson ran for a seat in the Texas House of Representatives. In that job, Sen. Hutchinson worked with other representatives to make laws that would help people in Texas. She worked as a state representative for four years.

2. Sen. Hutchinson is a hard working person who has constantly worked to improve her career. In 1976, she was given a chance to be the head of a board that worked to find safer ways to travel in the United States. She left Texas to work on the safety board, which was in Washington, D.C. In 1990, she was elected as the Texas State Treasurer, the same job that Gov. Richards had been elected to years earlier. As the state treasurer she cut the budget and fought against additional taxes. Then, in 1993, Sen. Hutchinson won a special election and was awarded one of two U.S. Senate seats. In 1994, she won a full six-year term in the U.S. Senate.

3. Sen. Hutchison has worked hard as a senator. She worked to fix laws that changed the way money was spent for the military. She also wrote and helped pass a law that regulated shipping on the oceans. Sen. Hutchison also worked to give veterans and people who retired from the military health care benefits. In 2006, she was elected for a third time as a U.S. Senator.

13. What kind of degree did Sen. Hutchinson get in 1967?

    a. Master's degree
    b. Doctoral degree
    c. Law degree
    d. Medical degree

14. What did Sen. Hutchinson do for a job before she ran for a seat in the Texas House of Representatives in 1972?

    a. Mother
    b. TV news reporter
    c. Lawyer
    d. State treasurer

15. What is the main topic of paragraph 3?

    a. Sen. Hutchinson's life before becoming a senator
    b. Sen. Hutchinson's accomplishments as a state treasurer
    c. Sen. Hutchinson's family
    d. Sen. Hutchinson's accomplishments as a senator

16. What does "Sen." mean?

    a. Senator
    b. Sent
    c. Sentry
    d. Sensor

Questions 17-20 pertain to both passages: "Ann Richards: The First Woman Governor of Texas" and "Kay Bailey Hutchinson: The First Woman Senator of Texas":

17. Why are Gov. Richards and Sen. Hutchinson famous?

    a. They were the first men to be governor and a U.S. senator in Texas
    b. They were the first women to be governor and a U.S. senator in Texas
    c. They were the first women to be teachers and news reporters in Texas
    d. They were the first women to have jobs outside of Texas

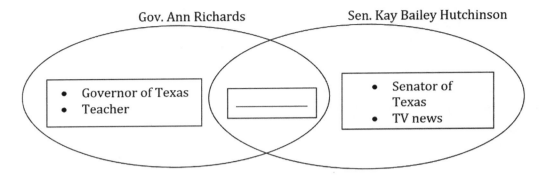

Gov. Ann Richards — Sen. Kay Bailey Hutchinson

- Governor of Texas
- Teacher

_____

- Senator of Texas
- TV news

18. What word belongs in the blank spot?

    a. Senator
    b. Governor
    c. State treasurer
    d. News reporter

19. Which woman is still working in government?

    a. Ann Richards
    b. Kay Bailey Hutchinson
    c. Both
    d. Neither

20. Why do you think the author wrote about these women?

    a. To show that women can have the same opportunities as men in Texas
    b. To explain the way government works in Texas
    c. To show Gov. Richards's funny side
    d. To show that men have the same opportunities as women in Texas

Questions 21 – 30 pertain to the following passage:

A Trip to Pavarti's House

Pavarti and Sam are in the same fifth-grade class at school. It is almost Halloween and Pavarti invited Sam to come to her house that weekend to carve pumpkins.

Pavarti (answering the phone): Hello?

Sam: Hello, is this Pavarti?

Pavarti: Yes, is this Sam?

Sam: Yes. Mom said I could come to your house tomorrow. She wanted to know what time would be good to drop me off.

Pavarti: We're going to buy the pumpkins in the morning and start carving after lunch. Why don't you come around 2 o'clock?

Sam: Sounds good. Mom wants to know how to get to your house. What is your address?

Pavarti: We live in town, at 145 State Street. Where do you live?

Sam: We're just outside of town on Route 20, at the intersection of Townline Road.

Pavarti: Take Townline Road north toward town. After two miles you will turn right on Elm Street.

Sam: Okay, I'm writing this down. Two miles, turn right on Elm Street.

Pavarti: Good. You will pass two traffic lights. At the third traffic light you will turn left to get on Rio Turnpike. Go about half a mile until you see a 7-Eleven on the right. The next street after the 7-Eleven is Main Street. Turn right onto Main Street.

Sam: Wait, wait, I want to make sure I get this right. Left on Rio Turnpike, at third traffic light. Go right at the 7-Eleven, half-mile down the road. It is Main Street.

Pavarti: That's right.

Sam: Where is your house after I turn onto Main Street?

Pavarti: We're all the way on the other end of the street. However, Main Street is one-way and you can't get to our house from the other end. Go past five streets. Our house is on the right side, in the middle of the sixth block.

Sam: (Writing it down) House is in the middle of the sixth block.

Pavarti: Yes. It is yellow and has a garage on the left. It is between a green house and a white house. It is the only yellow house on my block. Do not look for the address. It is very small and attached to the door in a crooked kind of way. It's really hard to see.

Sam: Okay, okay, let me write this down. Only yellow house on the block, between green and white houses.

Pavarti: Right. And there will be one or two cars in the driveway. Look for either a red truck or a small black car.

Sam: I have it all down. Our car is a white minivan. Hopefully you will not see it go by your house more than once!

Pavarti: (laughing) You should be fine. If you do get lost, just call us: 555-678-9101.

Sam: Sounds good. Hopefully we won't need it. Should I bring anything tomorrow?

Pavarti: Just your pumpkin carving skills. See you around 2 o'clock!

21. What is the main purpose of the telephone conversation?
    a. To arrange a pumpkin shopping trip
    b. To give Sam directions to Pavarti's house
    c. To arrange a Halloween party at Sam's house
    d. To give Pavarti directions to Sam's house

22. Pavarti is having Sam over. Why did Pavarti ask Sam where she lived?

    a. So Pavarti could give Sam directions from her own house
    b. So Pavarti could someday go to Sam's house
    c. So Pavarti could find out whether Sam lives in town
    d. So Pavarti could give directions to the closest 7-Eleven store

23. After Townline Road, what street does Sam's mother need to turn right onto?

    a. Rio Turnpike
    b. Main Street
    c. Route 20
    d. Elm Street

24. Why did Pavarti tell Sam the color of her house and the colors of the houses next to it instead of letting Sam use the address?

    a. Because the address is hard to see from the road
    b. Because Sam cannot read numbers
    c. Because Pavarti does not know her address
    d. Because the address is easy to see from the road

25. Why was Sam writing down Pavarti's spoken directions?

    a. To complete a school assignment
    b. So she would know how to carve pumpkins
    c. To show Pavarti how well she gives directions
    d. To remember Pavarti's directions to her house

26. According to Pavarti, what direction should Sam's mother take if she enters at the bottom of the Rio Turnpike shown below?

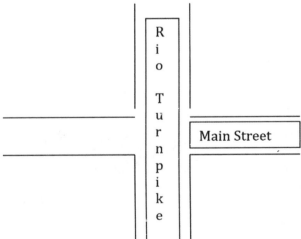

    a. Straight, then right
    b. Left, then straight
    c. Straight, then left
    d. Left, then right

- 58 -

27. What did Sam mean when she said about her family's white minivan, "Hopefully you won't see it go by more than once!"?

    a. Sam is hoping they don't drive the wrong way on Main Street
    b. Sam is hoping they don't get lost and have to drive up and down Main Street
    c. Sam is hoping Pavarti sees their car go by once
    d. Sam is hoping the car doesn't break down

28. Sam wrote down the following notes while Pavarti was giving directions:

- 3 traf lghts. L on Rio Turnpk
- 7-Eleven on right, 1/2-mile down
- Main Street

What part of Pavarti's directions did Sam write down?

    a. Take Townline Road north towards town. After two miles you will turn right on Elm Street
    b. It is yellow and has a garage on the left. It is between a green house and a white house. It is the only yellow house on my block
    c. Main Street is one way and you can't get to our house from the other end. Go past five streets
    d. At the third traffic light you will turn left onto Rio Turnpike. Go about half a mile until you see a 7-Eleven on the right. The next street after the 7-Eleven is Main Street

29. Tone in conversation describes the feelings or impressions a speaker gives to the listener. Some examples of tone are happy, sad, polite, and angry. What is the tone of this phone conversation?

    a. Angry
    b. Friendly
    c. Silly
    d. Rude

30. The following is Pavarti's morning schedule. What activity goes in the blank space?

    a. Take a nap
    b. Pick up Sam
    c. Give Sam directions
    d. Have lunch

Questions 31 – 35 pertain to the following passage:

Simon and Pedro's Shopping Trip

1. "Simon, where are you going?" asked Pedro. "You're missing your favorite show."

Pedro had just arrived at Simon's house on his bicycle. He had ridden over to see what his best friend was doing on a Saturday morning at 10 o'clock. Simon was usually watching cartoons around this time.

"I'm heading to the store," said Simon. "I've saved my allowance and I finally have enough money to buy the model plane I've wanted."

2. "Great!" said Pedro. "Can I come with you? I want to see it. Also, can I help you build it when we get back?"

"Sure," said Simon. "Let's go!"

3. Simon and Pedro rode down the street and turned right onto the highway. The hobby store, which sold model planes, cars, and other model vehicles, was just a few hundred yards down the road. At the store Simon and Pedro took some time to look at the other models on the shelves.

4. "Look!" said Pedro. "Here is a 1969 Mustang! It's $40! My dad said my grandfather used to own a real one. He bought it new and kept it for years. Then his brother, my uncle, bought it from him. Dad wishes he had never sold it."

5. "Really?" said Simon. "I'd love to ride in one of those. Look at this! A C17! Man, I'd get this instead, but it's $50 and I only have $30."

"What kind of plane were you planning to buy?" asked Pedro.

"The model of that B17G Flying Fortress," said Simon. "I have just enough to buy it."

"How much is it?" asked Pedro.

"It costs about $25," said Simon. "But I also have to pay for the sales tax."

"How much is tax?" asked Pedro.

"Eight percent," said Simon. "My mom figured it out for me. It's $2. That leaves me with $3 change."

"Do you get everything you need in the kit…like glue?" asked Pedro.

"Good question," said Simon. "I'll ask."

6. Simon went over to the clerk with the model airplane box in his hands. Pedro watched as the clerk nodded. He was hopeful that meant good news.

"Yes," said Simon, walking back to Pedro. "Everything is included."

"Well," said Pedro. "Let's head home and start building! When we're done, we'll break open my piggy bank and go buy the 1969 Mustang. Then we can play car chase."

"Excellent!" said Simon, as he headed toward the counter with the box and his wallet.

31. Why was Pedro surprised to find Simon outside on his bicycle on Saturday morning?
    a. Because Simon was usually watching cartoons
    b. Because Simon was usually still in bed
    c. Because Simon was grounded
    d. Because Simon had $30

32. What was the model that Pedro noticed in the store?

    a. C17
    b. B17G Flying Fortress
    c. 1969 Mustang
    d. A18H Flying Dutchman

33. What model did Simon want to buy, but couldn't afford?

    a. C17
    b. B17G Flying Fortress
    c. 1969 Mustang
    d. A18H Flying Dutchman

34. How much will Simon's model cost with tax?

    a. $25
    b. $27
    c. $45
    d. $50

35. What did Simon and Pedro plan to do after Simon bought his model?

    a. Buy the 1969 Mustang too and build both of them together
    b. Build the 1969 Mustang and then build the C17
    c. Build the B17G Flying Fortress and then go buy the 1969 Mustang
    d. Buy the 1969 Mustang and then build the B17G Flying Fortress

The following poem pertains to questions 36-38.

"Since Hanna Moved Away" by Judith Viorst

The tires on my bike are flat.
The sky is grouchy gray.
At least it sure feels like that
Since Hanna moved away.

Chocolate ice cream tastes like prunes.
December's come to stay.
They've taken back the Mays and Junes
Since Hanna moved away.

36. What is the overall tone of the poem?

    a. Excitement
    b. Regret
    c. Anger
    d. Grief

37. What is the main literary device used throughout this poem?

    a. Hyperbole
    b. Metaphor
    c. Repetition
    d. Foreshadowing

38. In the second stanza, what does it mean when the author writes "They've taken back the Mays and Junes?"

    a. The time has flown by and she missed out on the summer months.
    b. The summer months didn't feel as fun as they should have.
    c. When Hanna moved away, the weather turned cold.
    d. The narrator lost May and June to summer school.

Answer Key and Explanations for Test #2

TEKS Standard §110.7(3)(B) and (6)(F)

1. B: The expression "rain came down in sheets" means it was raining so hard that the rain looked like it was coming down in one solid sheet rather than separate drops.

TEKS Standard §110.7(7)(C)

2. D: Mona and Yuri's mother was asleep after having worked overnight as a nurse.

TEKS Standard §110.7(7)(C)

3. C: Mona and Yuri's mother goes to bed around 7 a.m. after working all night. She usually gets up after eight hours of sleep, which would be around 3 p.m.

TEKS Standard §110.7(7)(C)

4. A: War is a card game. It can be played with an ordinary deck of playing cards.

TEKS Standard §110.7(7)(C)

5. A: When a regular deck of playing cards is used, an ace has the highest value in War and beats all other cards.

TEKS Standard §110.7(7)(C)

6. B: To have a "war" in the card game War, both players have to have the same card.

TEKS Standard §110.7(7)(C) and (8)(B)

7. C: Mona won the first game that she and Yuri played. That is why Yuri said, "Beginner's luck."

TEKS Standard §110.7(6)(F)

8. A: When she said, "Actually, this game is all luck," Mona meant that the game did not require any skill to win. It just depended on the cards the players had.

TEKS Standard §110.7(6)(H)

9. A: Mona wins the round. A king is the second highest card in the deck. A jack is the fourth highest.

TEKS Standard §110.7(7)(C)

10. C: Gov. Richards taught social studies and history before getting into politics.

TEKS Standard §110.7(7)(D) and (9)(D)(i)

11. D: Paragraph 3 is mostly about Gov. Richards's achievements as governor of Texas.

TEKS Standard §110.7(3)(B)

12. A: Gov. Richards was joking about how stiff her hair was because of all the hairspray in it.

TEKS Standard §110.7(7)(C)

13. C: Sen. Hutchinson earned a law degree from the University of Texas in 1967.

TEKS Standard §110.7(7)(C)

14. B: Sen. Hutchinson worked as a TV news reporter before going into politics.

TEKS Standard §110.7(7)(D) and (9)(D)(i)

15. D: Paragraph 3 is mostly about Sen. Hutchinson's accomplishments while serving as a senator.

TEKS Standard §110.7(3)(B)

16. A: The abbreviation Sen. means Senator.

TEKS Standard §110.7(6)(E) and (7)(C)

17. B: Gov. Richards and Sen. Hutchinson were the first women to be governor and a U.S. senator in Texas.

TEKS Standard §110.7(6)(H) and (9)(D)(ii)

18. C: Both women served as the Texas State Treasurer before getting more important positions in government.

TEKS Standard §110.7(7)(C)

19. B: Sen. Hutchinson is still working as a U.S. Senator. Gov. Richards died in 2006, and the passage states that she left politics.

TEKS Standard §110.7(10)(A)

20. A: The author wrote these articles to show that women can have the same opportunities as men in Texas.

TEKS Standard §110.7(7)(C) and (9)(D)(i)

21. B: Sam called Pavarti to get directions to Pavarti's house. Sam will give the directions to her mother when they drive over the next day.

TEKS Standard §110.7(6)(H) and (7)(C)

22. A: Pavarti asked Sam where she lived so that she could give Sam directions from her own house.

TEKS Standard §110.7(7)(C)

23. D: Sam's mother will need to turn onto Elm Street after Townline Road.

TEKS Standard §110.7(7)(C)

24. A: Pavarti told Sam the color of her house and the houses around it because her address is hard to see from the road.

TEKS Standard §110.7(6)(H)

25. D: Sam was writing down what Pavarti was saying so that she would remember the directions the next day when she needed them.

TEKS Standard §110.7(7)(C) and (9)(D)(ii)

26. A: Sam's mother should go straight on Rio Turnpike before taking a right on Main Street.

TEKS Standard §110.7(3)(B) and (6)(F)

27. B: Sam is hoping that her and her mother don't get lost and have to drive up and down Main Street, especially since it runs only one way.

TEKS Standard §110.7(7)(C), (7)(D), and (9)(D)(ii)

28. D: Sam's notes written out would look like the following: At the third traffic light you will turn left onto Rio Turnpike. Go about half a mile until you see a 7-Eleven on the right. The next street after the 7-Eleven is Main Street.

TEKS Standard §110.7(10)(E)

29. B: The tone of Sam and Pavarti's telephone conversation is friendly.

TEKS Standard §110.7(7)(C) and (9)(D)(ii)

30. D: After buying the pumpkins, Pavarti's family is planning to have lunch before starting to carve them.

TEKS Standard §110.7(7)(C)

31. A: Simon was usually inside the house watching cartoons on Saturday morning.

TEKS Standard §110.7(7)(C)

32. C: Pedro noticed the model of the 1969 Mustang because his father had talked about that type of car.

TEKS Standard §110.7(7)(C)

33. A: Simon wanted to buy a model of a C17 fighter plane, but he didn't have enough money.

TEKS Standard §110.7(7)(C) and (6)(H)

34. B: Altogether, with tax, Simon had to pay $27.

TEKS Standard §110.7(7)(C), (8)(B), and (8)(C)

35. C: After buying Simon's model, the B17G Flying Fortress, they planned to build it and then go buy the 1969 Mustang that Pedro wanted and build that one as well.

TEKS Standard §110.7(9)(B)

36. D: The overall tone or mood of the poem is grief. The narrator is missing her friend who moved away and uses language that reflects deep pain at losing a friend. Nothing that she previously enjoyed doing, such as biking and eating ice cream, is as fun without her friend present.

TEKS Standard §110.7(9)(B) and (10)(E)

37. A: The main literary device used throughout the poem is hyperbole, which is a dramatic exaggeration. The main character's tires on her bike are unlikely to always be flat and chocolate probably did not literally taste like prunes to her. There is some repetition of language throughout the poem, but not enough to say it was the main device used. Foreshadowing is wrong because the event that this poem is focused on took place in the past. Metaphor is wrong because the narrator is not saying that her chocolate ice cream *is* prunes or calling one thing another in a metaphor.

TEKS Standard §110.7(9)(B) and (6)(E)

38. B: Throughout the poem, the narrator describes things she liked doing with her friend Hanna, such as eating ice cream and riding bikes. In the second stanza, the author says that "December's come to stay," and that "They've taken back the Mays and Junes," implying that her favorite things she did with Hanna were summer activities. It is implied that even though she still could do the fun things, such as eating ice cream and riding bikes, she doesn't want to without her friend, so it might as well be winter.

How to Overcome Test Anxiety

Just the thought of taking a test is enough to make most people a little nervous. A test is an important event that can have a long-term impact on your future, so it's important to take it seriously and it's natural to feel anxious about performing well. But just because anxiety is normal, that doesn't mean that it's helpful in test taking, or that you should simply accept it as part of your life. Anxiety can have a variety of effects. These effects can be mild, like making you feel slightly nervous, or severe, like blocking your ability to focus or remember even a simple detail.

If you experience test anxiety—whether severe or mild—it's important to know how to beat it. To discover this, first you need to understand what causes test anxiety.

Causes of Test Anxiety

While we often think of anxiety as an uncontrollable emotional state, it can actually be caused by simple, practical things. One of the most common causes of test anxiety is that a person does not feel adequately prepared for their test. This feeling can be the result of many different issues such as poor study habits or lack of organization, but the most common culprit is time management. Starting to study too late, failing to organize your study time to cover all of the material, or being distracted while you study will mean that you're not well prepared for the test. This may lead to cramming the night before, which will cause you to be physically and mentally exhausted for the test. Poor time management also contributes to feelings of stress, fear, and hopelessness as you realize you are not well prepared but don't know what to do about it.

Other times, test anxiety is not related to your preparation for the test but comes from unresolved fear. This may be a past failure on a test, or poor performance on tests in general. It may come from comparing yourself to others who seem to be performing better or from the stress of living up to expectations. Anxiety may be driven by fears of the future—how failure on this test would affect your educational and career goals. These fears are often completely irrational, but they can still negatively impact your test performance.

> **Review Video: <u>3 Reasons You Have Test Anxiety</u>**
> Visit mometrix.com/academy and enter code: 428468

Elements of Test Anxiety

As mentioned earlier, test anxiety is considered to be an emotional state, but it has physical and mental components as well. Sometimes you may not even realize that you are suffering from test anxiety until you notice the physical symptoms. These can include trembling hands, rapid heartbeat, sweating, nausea, and tense muscles. Extreme anxiety may lead to fainting or vomiting. Obviously, any of these symptoms can have a negative impact on testing. It is important to recognize them as soon as they begin to occur so that you can address the problem before it damages your performance.

> **Review Video: 3 Ways to Tell You Have Test Anxiety**
> Visit mometrix.com/academy and enter code: 927847

The mental components of test anxiety include trouble focusing and inability to remember learned information. During a test, your mind is on high alert, which can help you recall information and stay focused for an extended period of time. However, anxiety interferes with your mind's natural processes, causing you to blank out, even on the questions you know well. The strain of testing during anxiety makes it difficult to stay focused, especially on a test that may take several hours. Extreme anxiety can take a huge mental toll, making it difficult not only to recall test information but even to understand the test questions or pull your thoughts together.

> **Review Video: How Test Anxiety Affects Memory**
> Visit mometrix.com/academy and enter code: 609003

Effects of Test Anxiety

Test anxiety is like a disease—if left untreated, it will get progressively worse. Anxiety leads to poor performance, and this reinforces the feelings of fear and failure, which in turn lead to poor performances on subsequent tests. It can grow from a mild nervousness to a crippling condition. If allowed to progress, test anxiety can have a big impact on your schooling, and consequently on your future.

Test anxiety can spread to other parts of your life. Anxiety on tests can become anxiety in any stressful situation, and blanking on a test can turn into panicking in a job situation. But fortunately, you don't have to let anxiety rule your testing and determine your grades. There are a number of relatively simple steps you can take to move past anxiety and function normally on a test and in the rest of life.

> **Review Video: How Test Anxiety Impacts Your Grades**
> Visit mometrix.com/academy and enter code: 939819

Physical Steps for Beating Test Anxiety

While test anxiety is a serious problem, the good news is that it can be overcome. It doesn't have to control your ability to think and remember information. While it may take time, you can begin taking steps today to beat anxiety.

Just as your first hint that you may be struggling with anxiety comes from the physical symptoms, the first step to treating it is also physical. Rest is crucial for having a clear, strong mind. If you are tired, it is much easier to give in to anxiety. But if you establish good sleep habits, your body and mind will be ready to perform optimally, without the strain of exhaustion. Additionally, sleeping well helps you to retain information better, so you're more likely to recall the answers when you see the test questions.

Getting good sleep means more than going to bed on time. It's important to allow your brain time to relax. Take study breaks from time to time so it doesn't get overworked, and don't study right before bed. Take time to rest your mind before trying to rest your body, or you may find it difficult to fall asleep.

Review Video: The Importance of Sleep for Your Brain
Visit mometrix.com/academy and enter code: 319338

Along with sleep, other aspects of physical health are important in preparing for a test. Good nutrition is vital for good brain function. Sugary foods and drinks may give a burst of energy but this burst is followed by a crash, both physically and emotionally. Instead, fuel your body with protein and vitamin-rich foods.

Also, drink plenty of water. Dehydration can lead to headaches and exhaustion, especially if your brain is already under stress from the rigors of the test. Particularly if your test is a long one, drink water during the breaks. And if possible, take an energy-boosting snack to eat between sections.

Review Video: How Diet Can Affect your Mood
Visit mometrix.com/academy and enter code: 624317

Along with sleep and diet, a third important part of physical health is exercise. Maintaining a steady workout schedule is helpful, but even taking 5-minute study breaks to walk can help get your blood pumping faster and clear your head. Exercise also releases endorphins, which contribute to a positive feeling and can help combat test anxiety.

When you nurture your physical health, you are also contributing to your mental health. If your body is healthy, your mind is much more likely to be healthy as well. So take time to rest, nourish your body with healthy food and water, and get moving as much as possible. Taking these physical steps will make you stronger and more able to take the mental steps necessary to overcome test anxiety.

Review Video: How to Stay Healthy and Prevent Test Anxiety
Visit mometrix.com/academy and enter code: 877894

Mental Steps for Beating Test Anxiety

Working on the mental side of test anxiety can be more challenging, but as with the physical side, there are clear steps you can take to overcome it. As mentioned earlier, test anxiety often stems from lack of preparation, so the obvious solution is to prepare for the test. Effective studying may be the most important weapon you have for beating test anxiety, but you can and should employ several other mental tools to combat fear.

First, boost your confidence by reminding yourself of past success—tests or projects that you aced. If you're putting as much effort into preparing for this test as you did for those, there's no reason you should expect to fail here. Work hard to prepare; then trust your preparation.

Second, surround yourself with encouraging people. It can be helpful to find a study group, but be sure that the people you're around will encourage a positive attitude. If you spend time with others who are anxious or cynical, this will only contribute to your own anxiety. Look for others who are motivated to study hard from a desire to succeed, not from a fear of failure.

Third, reward yourself. A test is physically and mentally tiring, even without anxiety, and it can be helpful to have something to look forward to. Plan an activity following the test, regardless of the outcome, such as going to a movie or getting ice cream.

When you are taking the test, if you find yourself beginning to feel anxious, remind yourself that you know the material. Visualize successfully completing the test. Then take a few deep, relaxing breaths and return to it. Work through the questions carefully but with confidence, knowing that you are capable of succeeding.

Developing a healthy mental approach to test taking will also aid in other areas of life. Test anxiety affects more than just the actual test—it can be damaging to your mental health and even contribute to depression. It's important to beat test anxiety before it becomes a problem for more than testing.

> **Review Video: Test Anxiety and Depression**
> Visit mometrix.com/academy and enter code: 904704

Study Strategy

Being prepared for the test is necessary to combat anxiety, but what does being prepared look like? You may study for hours on end and still not feel prepared. What you need is a strategy for test prep. The next few pages outline our recommended steps to help you plan out and conquer the challenge of preparation.

Step 1: Scope Out the Test

Learn everything you can about the format (multiple choice, essay, etc.) and what will be on the test. Gather any study materials, course outlines, or sample exams that may be available. Not only will this help you to prepare, but knowing what to expect can help to alleviate test anxiety.

Step 2: Map Out the Material

Look through the textbook or study guide and make note of how many chapters or sections it has. Then divide these over the time you have. For example, if a book has 15 chapters and you have five days to study, you need to cover three chapters each day. Even better, if you have the time, leave an extra day at the end for overall review after you have gone through the material in depth.

If time is limited, you may need to prioritize the material. Look through it and make note of which sections you think you already have a good grasp on, and which need review. While you are studying, skim quickly through the familiar sections and take more time on the challenging parts. Write out your plan so you don't get lost as you go. Having a written plan also helps you feel more in control of the study, so anxiety is less likely to arise from feeling overwhelmed at the amount to cover.

Step 3: Gather Your Tools

Decide what study method works best for you. Do you prefer to highlight in the book as you study and then go back over the highlighted portions? Or do you type out notes of the important information? Or is it helpful to make flashcards that you can carry with you? Assemble the pens, index cards, highlighters, post-it notes, and any other materials you may need so you won't be distracted by getting up to find things while you study.

If you're having a hard time retaining the information or organizing your notes, experiment with different methods. For example, try color-coding by subject with colored pens, highlighters, or post-it notes. If you learn better by hearing, try recording yourself reading your notes so you can listen while in the car, working out, or simply sitting at your desk. Ask a friend to quiz you from your flashcards, or try teaching someone the material to solidify it in your mind.

Step 4: Create Your Environment

It's important to avoid distractions while you study. This includes both the obvious distractions like visitors and the subtle distractions like an uncomfortable chair (or a too-comfortable couch that makes you want to fall asleep). Set up the best study environment possible: good lighting and a comfortable work area. If background music helps you focus, you may want to turn it on, but otherwise keep the room quiet. If you are using a computer to take notes, be sure you don't have any other windows open, especially applications like social media, games, or anything else that could distract you. Silence your phone and turn off notifications. Be sure to keep water close by so you stay hydrated while you study (but avoid unhealthy drinks and snacks).

Also, take into account the best time of day to study. Are you freshest first thing in the morning? Try to set aside some time then to work through the material. Is your mind clearer in the afternoon or evening? Schedule your study session then. Another method is to study at the same time of day that you will take the test, so that your brain gets used to working on the material at that time and will be ready to focus at test time.

Step 5: Study!

Once you have done all the study preparation, it's time to settle into the actual studying. Sit down, take a few moments to settle your mind so you can focus, and begin to follow your study plan. Don't give in to distractions or let yourself procrastinate. This is your time to prepare so you'll be ready to fearlessly approach the test. Make the most of the time and stay focused.

Of course, you don't want to burn out. If you study too long you may find that you're not retaining the information very well. Take regular study breaks. For example, taking five minutes out of every hour to walk briskly, breathing deeply and swinging your arms, can help your mind stay fresh.

As you get to the end of each chapter or section, it's a good idea to do a quick review. Remind yourself of what you learned and work on any difficult parts. When you feel that you've mastered the material, move on to the next part. At the end of your study session, briefly skim through your notes again.

But while review is helpful, cramming last minute is NOT. If at all possible, work ahead so that you won't need to fit all your study into the last day. Cramming overloads your brain with more information than it can process and retain, and your tired mind may struggle to recall even previously learned information when it is overwhelmed with last-minute study. Also, the urgent nature of cramming and the stress placed on your brain contribute to anxiety. You'll be more likely to go to the test feeling unprepared and having trouble thinking clearly.

So don't cram, and don't stay up late before the test, even just to review your notes at a leisurely pace. Your brain needs rest more than it needs to go over the information again. In fact, plan to finish your studies by noon or early afternoon the day before the test. Give your brain the rest of the day to relax or focus on other things, and get a good night's sleep. Then you will be fresh for the test and better able to recall what you've studied.

Step 6: Take a practice test

Many courses offer sample tests, either online or in the study materials. This is an excellent resource to check whether you have mastered the material, as well as to prepare for the test format and environment.

Check the test format ahead of time: the number of questions, the type (multiple choice, free response, etc.), and the time limit. Then create a plan for working through them. For example, if you have 30 minutes to take a 60-question test, your limit is 30 seconds per question. Spend less time on the questions you know well so that you can take more time on the difficult ones.

If you have time to take several practice tests, take the first one open book, with no time limit. Work through the questions at your own pace and make sure you fully understand them. Gradually work up to taking a test under test conditions: sit at a desk with all study materials put away and set a timer. Pace yourself to make sure you finish the test with time to spare and go back to check your answers if you have time.

After each test, check your answers. On the questions you missed, be sure you understand why you missed them. Did you misread the question (tests can use tricky wording)? Did you forget the information? Or was it something you hadn't learned? Go back and study any shaky areas that the practice tests reveal.

Taking these tests not only helps with your grade, but also aids in combating test anxiety. If you're already used to the test conditions, you're less likely to worry about it, and working through tests until you're scoring well gives you a confidence boost. Go through the practice tests until you feel comfortable, and then you can go into the test knowing that you're ready for it.

Test Tips

On test day, you should be confident, knowing that you've prepared well and are ready to answer the questions. But aside from preparation, there are several test day strategies you can employ to maximize your performance.

First, as stated before, get a good night's sleep the night before the test (and for several nights before that, if possible). Go into the test with a fresh, alert mind rather than staying up late to study.

Try not to change too much about your normal routine on the day of the test. It's important to eat a nutritious breakfast, but if you normally don't eat breakfast at all, consider eating just a protein bar. If you're a coffee drinker, go ahead and have your normal coffee. Just make sure you time it so that the caffeine doesn't wear off right in the middle of your test. Avoid sugary beverages, and drink enough water to stay hydrated but not so much that you need a restroom break 10 minutes into the test. If your test isn't first thing in the morning, consider going for a walk or doing a light workout before the test to get your blood flowing.

Allow yourself enough time to get ready, and leave for the test with plenty of time to spare so you won't have the anxiety of scrambling to arrive in time. Another reason to be early is to select a good seat. It's helpful to sit away from doors and windows, which can be distracting. Find a good seat, get out your supplies, and settle your mind before the test begins.

When the test begins, start by going over the instructions carefully, even if you already know what to expect. Make sure you avoid any careless mistakes by following the directions.

Then begin working through the questions, pacing yourself as you've practiced. If you're not sure on an answer, don't spend too much time on it, and don't let it shake your confidence. Either skip it and come back later, or eliminate as many wrong answers as possible and guess among the remaining ones. Don't dwell on these questions as you continue—put them out of your mind and focus on what lies ahead.

Be sure to read all of the answer choices, even if you're sure the first one is the right answer. Sometimes you'll find a better one if you keep reading. But don't second-guess yourself if you do immediately know the answer. Your gut instinct is usually right. Don't let test anxiety rob you of the information you know.

If you have time at the end of the test (and if the test format allows), go back and review your answers. Be cautious about changing any, since your first instinct tends to be correct, but make sure you didn't misread any of the questions or accidentally mark the wrong answer choice. Look over any you skipped and make an educated guess.

At the end, leave the test feeling confident. You've done your best, so don't waste time worrying about your performance or wishing you could change anything. Instead, celebrate the successful completion of this test. And finally, use this test to learn how to deal with anxiety even better next time.

Review Video: 5 Tips to Beat Test Anxiety
Visit mometrix.com/academy and enter code: 570656

Important Qualification

Not all anxiety is created equal. If your test anxiety is causing major issues in your life beyond the classroom or testing center, or if you are experiencing troubling physical symptoms related to your anxiety, it may be a sign of a serious physiological or psychological condition. If this sounds like your situation, we strongly encourage you to seek professional help.

Thank You

We at Mometrix would like to extend our heartfelt thanks to you, our friend and patron, for allowing us to play a part in your journey. It is a privilege to serve people from all walks of life who are unified in their commitment to building the best future they can for themselves.

The preparation you devote to these important testing milestones may be the most valuable educational opportunity you have for making a real difference in your life. We encourage you to put your heart into it—that feeling of succeeding, overcoming, and yes, conquering will be well worth the hours you've invested.

We want to hear your story, your struggles and your successes, and if you see any opportunities for us to improve our materials so we can help others even more effectively in the future, please share that with us as well. **The team at Mometrix would be absolutely thrilled to hear from you!** So please, send us an email (support@mometrix.com) and let's stay in touch.

If you'd like some additional help, check out these other resources we offer for your exam:

http://MometrixFlashcards.com/STAAR

Additional Bonus Material

Due to our efforts to try to keep this book to a manageable length, we've created a link that will give you access to all of your additional bonus material.

Please visit https://www.mometrix.com/bonus948/staarg5read to access the information.